Foundations and Issues
in Library and Information Science

Foundations and Issues in Library and Information Science

BRUCE A. SHUMAN

with assistance from
Carole J. McCollough
Joseph J. Mika

1992
LIBRARIES UNLIMITED, INC.
Englewood, Colorado

LIBRARIES UNLIMITED, INC.
P.O. Box 6633
Englewood, CO 80155-6633

Library of Congress Cataloging-in-Publication Data

Shuman, Bruce A.
    Foundations and issues in library and information science / Bruce
A. Shuman, with assistance of Carole J. McCollough, Joseph J. Mika.
    xv, 175p. 17x25 cm.
    Includes bibliographical references and index.
    ISBN 0-87287-942-9(pbk)
    1. Library science. 2. Information science. I. McCollough,
Carole J. II. Mika, Joseph J. III. Title.
Z665.S484 1992
020--dc20   91-36679
                                                CIP

For Bekki, Ben, Josh, Pammus, and Mom

Contents

Introduction

Most library and information science professionals will recall a course they were obliged to take (or may be taking now), normally at the onset of their graduate studies, bearing a title something like "The Library in Society," "Foundations of Librarianship," or even "History of Libraries." Such a course covers, in varying degrees, signal events in the history of libraries and information centers, together with salient current issues, conveniently divided into between ten and fifteen installments for class presentation.

In such a course, after history is covered, students are exposed to whatever "the profession" thinks students ought to know about the different aspects of library and information work and related environments, together with the persistent and troublesome issues applicable to library work. *The profession* refers generally to the collective and integrated knowledge, philosophy, lore, thought, and activities of a large number of "information professionals," including librarians, media specialists, information scientists, and others in similar jobs. Speaking of "the profession" also implies that there is some consensus or unity of opinion and philosophy. In actual practice, such a consensus is difficult to achieve because information professionals are diverse in their views.

Within the mandate to teach students (or at least expose them to) what they will need to know, there is, and always has been, a broad range of topics and coverage. Unfortunately, there is no standardization in teaching these topics as there is in other professional fields. Some academic programs in library and information science either do not require a course in "issues" or do not offer one at all, assuming that issues and concerns of the field will be raised and discussed in other, subject-oriented courses and that there are other, more important courses to be included in the "core" or requirements for the master's degree.

In those accredited schools that do offer issues courses, the range of topics covered is great and the amount of time given to individual topics varies. Current issues change, and various instructors emphasize issues differently depending on their personalities and proclivities. One instructor may emphasize library and information science history, while another prefers the history of books and reading or printing. Both subjects are part of a proper introduction to the new student's grasp of library and information science. A common rationale for teaching history as part of the master's degree coursework is that new (or prospective) information professionals need at least some understanding of how their profession began, where it has been, how it has evolved, its present concerns, and (to the extent that we can predict) where it is going.

Another instructor may conclude that a proper "intro" course prepares students for the technical demands of the automated environment. Still other instructors may give comparatively little weight to historical studies, not because history is unimportant but because the constraints of a fifteen-week course preclude prolonged treatment of any single aspect of the field.

The bottom line is that library and information science faculty, wherever course content decisions are discussed openly, seek to achieve some measure of consensus about the topics, issues, and other information-related matters that belong in an issues-oriented course. The instructor(s) charged with offering the course must attempt to sequence those topics and assign them relative importance in terms of time to be spent on them.

In some cases, students and faculty have the comparative luxury of a two-term introductory course to cover all the significant material, affording students a relatively leisurely inspection and discussion of course material. For the most part, however, a single term of variable length is all that is available to faculty members to indoctrinate and infuse the librarian's credo, philosophies, policies, and rich heritage into inquiring minds.

This book grew out of the author's dissatisfaction with previous contemporary texts for use in an introductory course. Accredited library and information science programs in the United States display a "patchwork quilt" of curricular arrangements, virtually no two alike. This is evidence of a puzzling lack of consistency. Law schools, for example, have standardized curricula, and all first-year law students must take courses in such basics as torts, contracts, and jurisprudence. An underlying assumption of this book is that the introductory course is important for beginning library and information science students and will serve as good philosophical and intellectual preparation for the courses and careers to come.

This book is intended to present some of the more salient and currently important concerns of library and information science. It is possible that some of the reader's pet concerns have been glossed over, distorted, or even omitted. The author's intention was to propose and discuss those issues he deemed important at the time of writing. Other writers would doubtless have chosen other issues. The ultimate judgment of this work's relevance and value should be whether it informs and instructs and whether the reader is enlightened.

Topics of interest to current and future information professionals continually arise, grow in importance and media coverage, become much discussed, peak, subside, sometimes resurface, or even disappear. Currency is important in works of this type, but currency decays rapidly upon publication. While some long-term issues are covered here, the reader must remember that the information profession is in continual and ceaseless flux. Many disciplines and fields of knowledge have contributed to accumulated knowledge in the library and information science profession. That which we call library and information science did not simply spring forth full-grown from someone's fertile imagination. It has developed slowly over the centuries and continues to change because many diverse minds and philosophies have gone into shaping its course. The library and information science profession is eclectic, borrowing liberally from other fields of research and inquiry. A wide variety of disciplines have contributed to the shape of our field:

- The social sciences include those disciplines that focus on people's life in groups: sociology, anthropology, economics, history, political science, education, criminology, law, etc.

- Library science may not be a "true" science in the sense of rigor, reproducibility, consistency, etc. However, philosophies, goals, objectives, patterns, standards, services, collections, and issues, all of which have evolved in this field, seem to qualify library science as a full-blown discipline. From library science have proceeded articulation, discussion, and debate over the issues that vex our practitioners.

- Information science, dealing with the collection, storage, processing, and dissemination of information in all its forms, has also contributed to the body of our profession's theory and practice. As emerging technology becomes more standard, information science becomes increasingly important as a component in the future of our field.

- Communication, expressed in the classic Shannon-Weaver model, is paraphrased as "Who says what to whom through what channel, with what effect?"[1] This model also contributes to the establishment and systematic exploration of library science. Viewing information provision as a series of transactions between two persons, each with different traits, expectations, and understandings, has clarified the task of getting the right information to the right person in the right way, the job of librarians since their profession began.

- Computer science, the study of automation and its various aspects and applications, has greatly affected information transfer. Improved design of machines that can interact with people and efforts to mitigate the difficulties arising when people and machines interact have contributed greatly to the effectiveness of information storage, organization, and transfer.

- Educational technology, the blending of pedagogical methodology with new technology, has provided audiovisual information and usage skills for library science practitioners. When information is not available in the desired format, these individuals are able to produce that format themselves.

  Library and information science, a dynamic profession, is still very much in search of itself, with new challenges arising all the time. It is literally never the same field two years (or even two months) in a row. Therefore, it seems entirely fitting that the content of an introductory issues course be ever changing also. Variety in the content keeps the students' first exposure to their intended profession current and keeps the members of the school's instructional faculty, who may offer the same course several times a year, from becoming bored with repetition of material.

While there are already several book-length texts treating the various aspects of professional philosophy, nomenclature, concerns, and lore, none may be considered definitive or adequate to a profession changing so rapidly. This text is designed to cover not only significant current issues (circa 1992) for library and information science professionals, but also both history and futuring. Janus-like, our profession must look both backward and forward. Readings, quotations, problems, and debates are provided on current topics. The conversational style is designed to make for easier reading than is common in works of such a genre and, it is hoped, will render these topics accessible, interesting and informative without unduly sacrificing information or substance.

SCOPE AND LIMITATIONS

The following subjects are covered:

1. Recent library and information science history, to show how the profession has arrived at its present position in society.

2. The role(s) of different types of libraries and information centers in society.

3. The various types of libraries and information centers, together with their differing goals, funding sources, audiences, services and collections, and personnel requirements.

4. Issues for the profession, grouped according to a general scheme by type of library or service area.

5. Alternative future directions for libraries of various types.

For reasons both of conciseness and focus, this work does not treat technical services issues nor issues concerned with library service to children and young adults, except as they pertain to libraries in schools. This book is primarily concerned with libraries in the United States. Libraries of foreign nations and comparative or international aspects of services and collections are beyond the scope of this book.

The choice of issues for discussion is necessarily selective. Unlike the author who proclaimed, "I've just written a five-volume history of the world. I would have written a one-volume history, but I just didn't have the time!" this author has carefully pared this book down to its present size. Some matters are intentionally omitted. The area of "issues" for information professionals is a wide-open, highly subjective, field. This book attempts to present a selection of unresolved issues for information professionals to confront, ponder, debate, and perhaps resolve — until new issues arise.

NOTES

[1] Claude E. Shannon and Warren Weaver. *The Mathematical Theory of Communication* (Urbana, Ill.: University of Illinois Press, 1949).

1

Libraries and Information in Society

SOCIETY AND ITS INSTITUTIONS

No library or information center exists in a vacuum; it exists within society. A scholarly definition of *society* is "a broadly inclusive social organization that possesses both functional and cultural autonomy and that dominates all other types of organization."[1] A simpler definition of society is "the totality of social relationships among human beings."[2] With qualifications, the term may refer to interactions of a social nature within a particular group or to a people sharing common characteristics. A society possesses shared common and unique cultural traits. At the same time, many groups within a society may hold numerous cultural ideas of their own that are not shared. Nevertheless, the common culture and its dominant social values and norms form a distinctive set of ideas unique to that society. For purposes of clarity, references to society in this book will refer to people who may be termed *Americans* by virtue of living in the United States as a geographical entity rather than as a homogeneous people who share common values (for it is demonstrable that we do not).

Society is also composed of social organizations within their environments. Such organizations consist of groups of people who come together to carry out common tasks or activities. As an example, a college or university may be defined as a collection of faculty, students, and administrators who are jointly engaged in the tasks of acquiring and disseminating knowledge. A society generally acts as a cooperative in which individuals voluntarily relinquish certain rights and freedoms in exchange for laws, rules, and protections. If, as expressed by many philosophers, the nature of man is aggressive and dangerous, then society is necessary to protect its members, especially the weak, from the strong. Society thus acts as a brake or safeguard, attempting to balance the wishes of competing individuals and interests by following the rule that the best policy is that which provides the greatest good for the greatest number. In a democratic society, where individuality is permitted and encouraged, competing interests lead to uneven benefits from society and to conflict over scarce or expensive resources. While this is unavoidable, a democratic society will attempt, through taxation, laws, and law enforcement, to provide a system that is "fair."

Society provides its members with, among other things, (1) social controls, (2) education, (3) livelihoods and useful roles, (4) socialization of new members, (5) values and shared experiences, (6) stratification, and (7) care for those unable to care for themselves. All societies provide such "services"; the primary differences are in the values attached to them. Each individual within a

1

society is motivated to meet basic needs and each makes contributions to that society in exchange for benefits, although both contributions and benefits vary with the individual.

THE LIBRARY AS A SOCIAL AGENCY

Our example of a social organization, an academic institution of higher learning, is defined as a collection of faculty, students, and administrators who are jointly engaged in the tasks of acquiring and disseminating knowledge. Another social organization, a library, is a collection of people whose aggregate function is that of acquiring, organizing, and disseminating knowledge and/or entertainment.

The library exists within society and interacts with it in many different ways. The function of the library within modern society has many definitions; just as there are many types of libraries, so there are many different functions. For example, it is the function of an academic or school library to serve the needs of students, while the public librarian must consider the wishes and expressed desires of all members of a community. Academic or school librarians may serve members of the surrounding community, but these persons are not the primary clientele.

Within our democratic society, the public library exists to satisfy citizens' information and entertainment needs as well as to maximize and protect their right to know. The public library is a social agency that has found a not-always-comfortable niche in society as a provider of materials and services that promote a sense of satisfaction with one's life. In any given community, however, only a comparatively small percentage of residents can justifiably refer to themselves as *library users*, however we define the term. Most citizens do not choose to make use of the library, getting along just fine (or thinking they do) without the comforts and opportunities offered by the public library. With a support base of only a fraction of the community, the library dependent upon public support must be aware that its survival is in jeopardy.

Special libraries – a vast array of facilities providing information and materials to special audiences – are another type of information agency. (Special libraries are discussed in chapter 8.) A special library, which is primarily or wholly devoted to a type of material or user, must be understood not to include special collections in academic or public libraries, in which special materials are segregated for the use of clients specifically seeking them.

COMMUNICATION AND THE LIBRARY

People come to libraries and information centers to borrow or use materials that will help them answer questions, write papers, prepare assignments, read in comparative quiet, consult sources beyond their financial means, or avail themselves of other provided services. Sometimes they come to attend or participate in programs, film showings, public speeches, debates, and story-hours. Others want to borrow audiovisual materials. Still others seek consumer information, stock quotes, tax assistance, trivia or current events facts, or recipes. What do these library and information needs have in common? Communication, the transmission of information from one person to another, or from one person to millions.

If the library or information center may be seen as a medium of communication, then librarians and information professionals will do well to develop effective communication skills. Some persons are born communicators, gifted with the ability to get ideas across to others, knowing how to talk to individuals and groups, to make listeners understand, and sometimes to influence or persuade. But others may have more difficulty conveying their ideas to others.

Communication frequently takes a silent form. A painting may speak forcefully to us, as may body language, signs, and gestures. But libraries and information professionals are in the business of promoting communication with and for their patrons and they require excellent verbal communication skills. Those persons who are not born with such skills may learn them through in-service workshops or through coursework in library school curricula. Communication skills can be developed and improved through practice and repetition.

Let us briefly consider the classic Shannon-Weaver model of a communication system.[3] Suppose that a communicator has a thought-picture in mind and desires to convey it to you so that you both share the same image. If people were clairvoyant or telepathic, there would be no problem of distortion or misunderstanding. The communicator would simply "beam" the thought at you and the two of you would share the same picture.

However, we are not a race of clairvoyants, and therefore, when others speak to you, their thoughts must be encoded into a message, using a commonly agreed-upon symbology, words. Words must have agreed-upon meanings, and establishing these meanings becomes a problem of sizeable proportions. The message must then be placed in a channel, such as soundwaves in the air, and transmitted to you, the receiver. You then decode the message into words, analyze their meanings, understand what has been said, and comprehend what is meant by it. Along the way, the message is vulnerable to enemies such as noise, body language, expectation, degree of attention, and other distractions, which tend to cloud, rob, or distort meaning. Additionally, our diverse backgrounds and life experiences tend to give each of us different interpretations of words themselves.

In view of these obstacles, it is perhaps amazing that effective communication happens at all! Still, libraries are ubiquitous communications centers, and librarians are charged with the difficult task of acquiring, storing, managing, and disseminating communication, which tasks they perform as best they can.

GOALS AND OBJECTIVES OF LIBRARIES

All libraries have goals; the wiser librarians articulate their goals carefully. To attempt to get along without stated goals, or to try to exist with amorphous, inchoate goals such as "we serve people," just won't cut it in today's world. There is an old institutional maxim that runs something like this: "Having lost sight of our objectives, we therefore redoubled our efforts." In other words, it doesn't matter how fast you're running if you don't know where you're going. Goals are necessary because if you don't know where you're going, how will you know when you get there? Setting of goals has become a primary management skill for librarians and information professionals. Enlightened managers now include all levels of staff in goal and role setting, from the highest level of administration down to the workers who perform blue-collar tasks.

Before goals are set, however, it is necessary to address the library's overall mission. The mission of the library may be seen as the visionary and long-range aim of its existence and the focus of all its efforts. Yet many library managers and staff members seem to have given inadequate consideration to the formulation of the institutional mission of the library.[4]

Remembering that our mission is the overall aim towards which the library or information center staff commit their efforts, resources, and personnel, everyone in the organization must understand that mission and work towards its furtherance. Critics maintain that the typical library or information center, unlike most for-profit enterprises, has yet to figure out what business it is actually in. Is the library in the book business, the information business, the entertainment industry, or the preservation business? And how, for example, does it feel about providing a part-time home for the homeless? A mission is not always easily decided, and lack of consensus may result in personnel working at cross-purposes.

Within the mission statement of the library or information center should be a number of more specific and less lofty goals that further that mission. These goals, which may vary in number, are in furtherance of the mission; achieving them helps fulfill the mission.

More specific than goals are measurable objectives for the library and information center, objectives whose fulfillment is seen to be in furtherance of the goals. The list of services to be provided should grow out of, and proceed from, these objectives. Services are manifestations of objectives, expressed as provisions to the patrons or users. As an example, if the library or information center has as its overall mission the maximization of community access to information and among the goals articulated is that of providing such access without regard to whether the patron is able to visit the library or not, a logical service becomes extension of library services to the homebound.

Each level is derived from the one above it and all efforts should work towards the achievement of the mission. Cutting across all levels of this hierarchical structure is one further component, that of constraints, which restrict and channel the capabilities of the institution. As a result of the primary outcome, of services and collections, the public reacts by means of feedback. Feedback, defined as the return of information from the users, consists of comments, requests, praise, criticisms, etc. Feedback frequently leads to changes in budgets, based upon the perception of whether satisfaction is expressed.

Each goal, which it should be possible to measure the accomplishment of, should be tested against all other goals, in the light of feedback from the community, to see if it is valid in both the economic and social senses. A change of goals will be dictated by economics, analysis of feedback, and experimentation.

As no two libraries are exactly alike, it is both natural and appropriate that to a certain extent they have differing goals and objectives. Their missions, however, will be similar, at least within one type of library. The goals of public libraries will vary with the environments in which they find themselves, but their missions will have a certain similarity across political and geographical jurisdictions.

In academic libraries, missions will vary directly and considerably with the overall institutional mission. For example, when the curriculum changes, so will (or should) the academic library's missions, goals, and objectives. School libraries and information centers are normally seen to reflect the overall missions of their school districts.

PHILOSOPHIES OF LIBRARIES

There are varying philosophical approaches within libraries and information centers (in public libraries, for example, there is a rivalry between the "demand" principle and the "prescriptive" one). Once there is some consensus on which services are to be provided, philosophical differences often arise over the appropriate levels of provision of those services. Funding is a significant determinant in deciding upon levels of service, but philosophy may be "liberal" or "conservative," or somewhere along a continuum encompassing a large, middle-of-the-road category.

The liberal approach to library provision means that the librarian accepts an active role in provision of information or materials. The staff will do anything within reason and financial ability to respond to the information need of the patron. Should this require placing a long-distance telephone call to obtain necessary information, the librarian does so without hesitation. When needed, a liberal library makes inquiries on behalf of patrons, as in the case of negotiating in English with a landlord on behalf of a Spanish-speaking tenant whose landlord does not supply adequate heating in the winter. Whereas another librarian might merely provide a telephone number or a name to ask for, the librarian in a liberal library acts as agent on behalf of the patron.

On the other hand, a conservative library plays a more passive role in dealing with people. The conservative philosophy, frequently dictated by a lack of money, requires that the library be open for business a certain number of hours each week and supply a standard number of basic library services to its clientele. Beyond that, few "extras" are supplied. For example, the conservative librarian may hesitate (if not outright refuse) to call city hall or another agency on behalf of a client. Not only is such service outside the scope of the library, but it may well be deemed politically risky to pursue such a course of action. When the conservative philosophy springs from fiscal restraint, even a telephone call outside the local zone or a brief long-distance call on behalf of a patron's request for information may be outside the library's range. Whether this approach is ultimately timid and derelict in its responsibility, or merely prudent, would depend on one's philosophy of library service and the circumstances in which a library finds itself. This philosophical dichotomy may also identify the ways in which services are offered, and to whom.

provide: patron:

IMAGES OF THE LIBRARIAN/
INFORMATION PROFESSIONAL

The professional image of the librarian needs improvement. *We* know that we're interesting people and that we play important roles in society. But how do we get everybody else to realize this and to improve their perceptions and attitudes? We are making progress in refurbishing our image, but in many ways our public relations task is as difficult as selling any product or service.

At varying times, and in the eyes of different individuals, librarians and information professionals are seen as educators, guides, civil servants, minor functionaries, media specialists, clerks, literary advisers, members of university faculty, babysitters, social workers, traffic cops, trivia specialists, bet-settlers, and propagandists for the dominant powers in society. Depending on the individual and the vantage point, any of these views may be valid, but the image the profession seeks to promote is that librarians are exciting and extremely clever people. They are resourceful, energetic, and frequently fascinating to talk to because of the breadth and range of their knowledge. They work long hours tirelessly for the betterment of society, doing work no other group of people can perform quite as well, and always place the public good ahead of merely financial rewards, which is just as well since they are chronically, almost universally, underpaid. They are skilled information professionals, who can quickly and efficiently compile a bibliography, consult a catalog, write an abstract, decipher an index, go online to find information, and bring a wealth of knowledge on virtually all subjects to a game of "Trivial Pursuit." Sometimes they act as unpaid social workers, trying to diagnose and refer the problems of those who walk through their doors. They serve as homework consultants, tutors, reader's advisers, guides to the literature of various subjects, teachers, babysitters, traffic cops, and referees, all without additional compensation. At times they are researchers, digging deeply into stored literature on behalf of people too busy to do their own digging, and sifting, interpreting, and presenting facts. They are opinion leaders, authorities on many topics, and the community's first line of defense against the forces of repression, censorship, reaction, and totalitarianism. They are change-agents, working quietly but with determination for a better world and striving to alter people's perceptions of the world around them.[5]

After this discussion of the underlying theories and important characteristics of library and information science professionals, we turn to the reasons for development of libraries and information centers as institutions. In limited space and with our focus on current issues, chapter 2 briefly reviews the past five decades of progress in the information services field.

NOTES

[1] Marvin E. Olson. *The Process of Social Organization* (New York: Holt, Rinehart and Winston, 1968), pp. 96-97.

[2] *The American Heritage Dictionary of the English Language* (Boston: Houghton-Mifflin, 1971).

[3] Claude E. Shannon and Warren Weaver. *The Mathematical Theory of Communication* (Urbana, Ill.: The University of Illinois Press, 1949), pp. 6-16.

[4] Much of this discussion is based on Charles H. Granger, "A Hierarchy of Objectives." *Harvard Business Review* (May 1964): 63-68.

[5] A recent example of stereotyping of librarians in popular literature may be seen in Stephen King's "The Library Policeman," one of four novellas in *Four Past Midnight* (New York: Viking, 1990).

REFERENCE LIST

Asheim, Lester. "Means and Ends in Librarianship." In Edelman, Hendrik, ed., *Libraries and Information Science in the Electronic Age*, pp. 100-111. Philadelphia: Institute for Scientific Information, 1986.

Becker, Joseph. "Libraries, Society and Technological Change." *Library Trends* (Winter 1979): 409-17.

Bell, Daniel. "The Social Framework of the Information Society." In Forester, Tom, ed., *The Microelectronics Revolution*, pp. 500-549. Cambridge, Mass.: MIT Press, 1980.

Landau, Herbert. "The Challenge of the Information Society: Are We Ready?" In Edelman, *Libraries and Information Science*, pp. 36-56.

Sapp, Gregg. "What the Librarian Didn't See in the Mirror: Aspects of the Professional Stereotype." *Catholic Library World* 58 (November/December 1986): 135-38.

Stam, David H., and Deirdre C. Stam. "Library." In *Funk & Wagnalls New Encyclopedia 16*, pp. 100-106. New York: Funk & Wagnalls, 1986.

Terkel, Studs. "Librarian." In *Working*, pp. 540-43. New York: Pantheon, 1974.

Be the mind of Society
defense

2 A Brief History of Information Issues

This chapter focuses not on "what" but on "why," as befits a work concerned with issues. After addressing some fundamental concerns connected with the development of record-keeping and record-keepers and a few salient events or people who have greatly influenced the progress of that record-keeping, we cover significant developments and problems of the past four or five decades in the arena of information provision, emphasizing controversial issues connected with progress in this area.

WHY STUDY THE PAST?

An appropriate question to be asked at the outset of a discussion of library history is "Why study the past?" After all, the past is dead. It cannot be changed in any real sense, so what's the point in poring over it? But it is often said that "those who do not study the past are bound to repeat it," and Alvin Toffler paraphrased that point in *Future Shock*: "True. But those who do not study the past may be forced to endure the future, which may be worse."[1] It is generally agreed upon by the library and information profession that a sense of history is requisite to an understanding of where our profession has come from, a sense of where it is today and how it got there, and even a clue as to the general direction in which we would like it to evolve. Only by studying its past can any profession have a sense of itself and where it is heading. In this chapter we consider the distant past insofar as libraries are involved in it and then cover the last half century.

THE ORIGINS AND DEVELOPMENT OF RECORD-KEEPING

Let us begin with an assertion: The human being is, and always has been, a record-keeping animal. People are possessed of the seemingly instinctive and inbred need to commit both their thoughts and their experiences to some sort of surface for preservation beyond the moment. All formal history proceeds from this innate human drive to set down a record of events.

In some societies, an oral tradition has prevailed, with legends and sagas about divine or human deeds told and retold through the generations from the old to the young. Even though they may not have had a written language or a tendency to commit feelings to writing or drawing surfaces, such tribes and social groups acted true to the human trait of recording events for the instruction, warning, or benefit of generations to come. Even such an oral tradition has characteristics of record-keeping, as generations have passed their wisdom, lore, customs, hopes, fears, warnings, and dreams on to the next generation, to be passed to the next, and so on to the present day. That the medium of preservation of cultural heritage has varied does not alter the point that record-keeping, through one medium or another, has been an integral part of each culture's society.

The Emergence of Recorded Information

The term *cave-man* is imprecise and heavily stereotyped, yet it is familiar to virtually any literate person in Western society. It is therefore used here as a convenient term for our common ancestors.

Evidence exists that record-keeping functions were extant in cave-man days, as amply shown by cave paintings that have endured in various parts of the world to the present day. Whether originally intended for decoration or to commemorate signal events in the life of the group, cave paintings show that the human need to record and preserve information has always been present. Paintings of animals, botanical shapes, people in the roles of hunters and gatherers, and even forces of nature adorn caves in most parts of the world, giving silent and enduring testimony to the urge common in all of us to inscribe events somehow and somewhere, before they are forgotten.

Libraries, if the term may be used here, have been around in one form or another since people first felt the need both to remember important information that exceeded short-term memory and to have such information readily accessible. Information has always been a valuable commodity. Cave-men had to know which plants and animals to eat and not to eat and which were apt to eat them. Initially, at least, vital facts were inbred into the human consciousness and orally taught or passed along to the young, so that the need for a physical storehouse or repository of vital information was not required.

Approximately 7,000 years ago, at least two forms of information were necessary for rulers to govern their realms and their people effectively in an increasingly complex world. These two forms of information dealt with the ramifications of religious observances and of tax collection.

As religion became increasingly more complicated, kings and high priests found it both necessary and desirable to write down in some form or another and thus preserve sacred writings. When an authoritative source of rules was needed, early "librarians" were frequently priests who maintained and interpreted the official files of religious observance for the unlettered. As soon as there were several such books to consult, a library was born.

The other wellspring from which libraries and information centers may be said to have come was financial interest, resulting from government awareness that some form of citizen contribution in the form of currency or revenue was both necessary and appropriate to the maintenance of government. The official designation and appointment of *someone*, whether called a priest, a librarian, or an accountant, was necessary for keeping the king's sums and figuring out who owed what each year. As the populations of nations grew and the desire for conquest and assimilation of neighboring or foreign land into one's own empire occupied the thoughts of kings, it became harder and harder to know what each citizen's "fair share" of the expenses of running government was without writing things down in ledgers of some kind. This called for a reasonably accurate census of taxable populations, some means of recording contributions and taxes paid, and a person to keep such accounts and retrieve information on demand. Another form of library had begun. From these two disparate beginnings, librarians emerged, acquiring collections containing history, religion, literature, philosophy, political science, social science, economics, medicine, etc.

Librarians originally were high-born and highly important people. Sometimes, when Pharaoh's priest who was entrusted with the keeping of records and religious observances walked or rode by, prudent civilians prostrated themselves, rising only when the "librarian" had passed, fearful of giving offense. Never before and never since has society accorded such rank and privilege to librarians as were found in pre-Hellenic Egypt.

But the focus of this book is on the present, not the past. Its scope is primarily the mid-to-late-twentieth century, for that is when many of the information-related issues that vex us now arose and proliferated, contemporaneously with new technologies. The rest of this chapter, therefore, touches upon only a few highlights of librarianship's formative past, then discusses library and information science history from the end of the Second World War in 1945 to the present day.

THE ALEXANDRIAN LIBRARY AND MATERIALS USED AND FOUND IN ANCIENT EGYPT

A relatively advanced civilization grew out of the fertile Nile River Valley in Egypt. Large libraries were made possible when tablets of stone and clay, which were cumbersome to use and time-consuming to employ, were supplanted, for the most part, by papyrus. Papyrus was easily grown by the banks of the river and comparatively cheaply produced through the interweaving or gluing together of papyrus reeds, making a crude but serviceable paper that could hold thousands of characters of writing. Papyrus did not possess the flexibility and suppleness of animal skins (vellum, which came from the skins of cattle or oxen, and parchment, made from sheep and goats) but it did not require slaughter of livestock and was much simpler to prepare and use. As stated earlier, libraries (in the Egyptian experience) began when Pharaoh and his priesthood needed to write down information. For economic, religious, social, and historical reasons the libraries thrived. In many Egyptian communities, they became the "center of life" as part of the temple in a society where church and state were one. There were two principal types of records, religious and commercial/financial. Papyrus was cheap and plentiful, as the climate favored the flooding of the Nile each year, leaving a narrow but verdant strip of alluvial land suitable to the growing of food crops and reeds, such as papyrus. The rest of the area was a "desert" of low humidity, good for preservation of records (as long as insects didn't discover them), one of the principal reasons why so many Egyptian records are preserved in the world's museums to the present day. What came to be the great Alexandrian library's catalog of holdings was originally carved onto one wall of a temple, for convenient reference, but after the number of holdings began to grow, there was neither space for nor interest in trying to get every new acquisition's "label" incised on the temple wall. A new system was needed, and the librarian priests of the temples and libraries invented a convenient system whereby like materials would be collected in bins on rolls of papyrus. Small scraps of papyrus would be inscribed with "tags" or a few significant words of the rolls' contents and the tags would be affixed to one end of the roll with a thong of leather, so that a browser or staff member could scan many rolls relatively quickly without the laborious and troublesome chore of opening rolls to see what they contained. Among subjects to be found in the larger, classified Egyptian libraries were state administration, religion, magic, myth, medicine, and science.

Pharaoh's "librarian" wore two hats, serving in his primary function as a high priest of the temple and acolyte of one or more gods. In the fourth century B.C., the conquest of Egypt by Alexander the Great had the effect of a "hostile takeover" of Egyptian scholarship, with the Hellenization of the Ptolemaic kings continuing for almost three centuries. The center of learning of Egyptian scholarship was a port city at the mouth of the Nile which Alexander, with characteristic modesty, renamed Alexandria in 332 B.C. In a comparatively short time, this library grew to be the greatest in the world.

In the third century B.C., a great research institute, museum, and library were established at Alexandria by Ptolemy I Soter (367-283 B.C.) with the help of Demetrius of Phaleron, originally a Greek scribe, whose objective was to demonstrate the superiority of the occupying Greek culture and community over the indigenous culture. In time, the Alexandrian became the "national library" of Greek Egypt, attempting to acquire a copy of every title in Greek. The acquisition methods employed might seem harsh to today's patrons. The Alexandrian library, it seems, was subject to a wave of nationalism, or chauvinism, in view of what it saw as competition from royal libraries established at about the same time in Macedonia and Pergamum. A law was therefore enacted that any traveler or tradesperson who brought a copy of any book (or scroll) into Alexandria was subject to having that work confiscated and copied by royal scribes. The original was retained to become a permanent part of the Alexandrian library, and the copy, when finally it was completed, returned to the original owner. Should the original owner be unwilling or unable to wait to have the book copied, the transaction was considered a donation to the people of Greek Egypt. In this manner, the great library grew apace and kept well ahead of its competition. There is no record of grumbling from the original owners of the books at the discovery that their property was forfeit and that the copy, when received, was likely to contain errors and sloppy workmanship; it was not considered prudent to voice objection to or criticism of the law, and it is extremely likely that complainers, having no recourse, stifled their discontent.

As a result of this aggressive acquisitions policy, the Alexandrian collection, in its halcyon years (the first century B.C.), consisted of over one-half million papyrus scrolls, with a main library located in Pharaoh's palace and a "branch" in the Temple of Sarapis, established by Ptolemy III, which stood until A.D. 391. But hungry insects, the combustibility of papyrus, and especially the tides and fortunes of political change all conspired to weaken or even destroy this great collection of knowledge. Over four centuries, the Alexandrian library was burned seven times. In 48 B.C., the main library at

Alexandria burned during the siege of Cleopatra's Egypt by Julius Caesar, during which a fire set at the docks and harbor spread to the library, destroying its contents.

But not all activity related to recorded information was confined to libraries. During the time of Julius and Augustus Caesar there was an active book trade in Alexandria. Callimachus at the Alexandrian library completed a comprehensive bibliography of Greek literature, "the Pinakes," in the second century B.C. which, though now lost, survived into the Byzantine period as a standard reference work.

Parchment was invented as the result of rivalry between Ptolemy V of Egypt and Eumenes II of Pergamum. Ptolemy, fearing that the library at Pergamum might surpass those of Alexandria despite the "copy and replace" law in force throughout Egypt, placed an embargo on papyrus, which grew profusely in the fertile Nile delta, and little or not at all in the more arid Tigris/Euphrates region around Pergamum. With the supply of papyrus drastically reduced, Eumenes was obliged to develop an industry in parchment for domestic use. Vellum and parchment proved to be much more supple and versatile than papyrus and facilitated development of the modern book (known as a codex) in the second century A.D. Anyone who has ever read a scroll (a modern-day example is the Torah, used in Jewish worship services) will appreciate the difference between scroll and codex in trying to get from page 1 to page 200. In a scroll it is necessary to unroll the pages from one stick while rolling onto the other (two hundred times) to arrive at the desired portion of the text. The codex, consisting of separate pages attached at one side and free on all others, permits a quick and easy turning from any page to any other page. This means that the development of pliable parchment, despite the problems of curing animal skins and working them into "pages," was a definite forward step in the progress of both books and libraries.

Other sources of "paper" existed up to and beyond the time of Ptolemy and Eumenes. At one time or another, stone, clay, parchment, vellum, tree bark, leaves, and linen rags were used as writing surfaces, with mixed results, in different parts of the world.

GUTENBERG: A GREAT LEAP FORWARD IN COMMUNICATION

Johannes Gutenberg (c.1400-1468), a German printer, is generally credited with changing the world forever through his technological triumph: printing from moveable metal type.* What that means is that it became possible to reproduce printed pages with metal instead of by writing. Gutenberg is believed to have printed his first book-length work, a bible in Latin, in the year 1455 in Mainz, Germany, although ownership of both his press and his business soon passed to a partner, Joachim Fust. Printing spread throughout Europe in a comparatively short time.

---

*Korean historians claim that their people were printing from handmade molds as early as A.D. 1000.

The printing press made possible several developments that changed communication forever. Books, reading, literacy, and, as Marshall McLuhan reminds us, standardization of language made it possible, for the first time in history, for people to read ... and to make grammatical mistakes.

Within twenty-five years, books became a common sight in the homes of Europeans, while printing and bookselling had become fairly common occupations. Once the common citizen could afford to own books, their collection into libraries was rapid and inevitable.

Of course, like almost all inventions, printing met with resistance. Numerous noble families in the countries to which printed books spread were proud to proclaim that they wouldn't have any printed books in their homes. But time and circumstances changed, and soon printed books were the common materials of society, while their handmade, hand-written counterparts became archival and museum artifacts.

Marshall McLuhan points out that books standardized language, which gave people a sense of their own common identity with others who spoke similarly. This gave rise, eventually, to in-group identification and corresponding intolerance of those who spoke differently. As a consequence, wars broke out between national groups, defined by the languages they spoke as natives, replacing the most frequent earlier causes of war: religious differences and heresy.[2]

WAR AND LIBRARIES

The "Fall of Rome" is recorded as occurring in the year A.D. 476, but it was a long, drawn-out process, which culminated in that year in a battle that proved decisive for the fate of the empire. After Rome had been conquered by illiterate Frankish tribes (who came to plunder and stayed to settle) reading, learning, and, of course, libraries (which had flourished under the Hellenic influence), began a long, steady decline within Roman society. Books were never banned or declared dangerous, they just lost their importance in daily life for most people, whose fortunes seemed tied to prevailing political and military factors. Libraries, therefore, were dispersed, with some dismantled, others destroyed, and still others moved eastward to Constantinople, or Byzantium, in Asia Minor, where "civilization" could still be said to be flourishing.

It is regrettable but true that conquerors have often used the power gained through conquest to censor the reading material of the conquered. Christians saw the fall of Rome as an opportunity to remove or revise reading material that did not agree with their beliefs and tenets. Later (from the seventh century onward), Muslims, who harried and attacked Roman territories from their bases in the Moorish Mediterranean, hated and feared classical learning as contrary to their faith and caused the destruction of innumerable books that were inconsistent with the teachings of the Koran.

Roman libraries, unlike those of Egypt, existed for the most part in moist climatic regions. The enemies of books and libraries (and, consequently, of preservation for posterity) of the period were political strife, fire, humidity, bugs, vermin, war, and conquest, along with illiteracy, religion, apathy, and popular trends, which seem to have favored or disfavored reading and libraries in cyclic patterns throughout the world's recorded history.

The effects of war on libraries are far-reaching and sometimes calamitous. As mentioned, conquering Moors found little use for books that disagreed with the Koran and tended to deal summarily with them. When Henry VIII broke away from the Roman Catholic Church and installed in its place an official Church of England, his armies confiscated as much "papist" literature as they could find and consigned it to the bonfire. There are reports that church bells of cathedrals and other buildings of Catholics who resisted Henry's new religious order were frequently melted down for cannons, which served the dual purpose of stifling dissent and building up the artillery strength of the king's armed forces.

Throughout history, conquered peoples frequently have suffered the loss (and often the destruction) of their books. It has long been a principle of conquest that if you wish to subjugate a people, you have to destroy their literature. So history teems with instances of libraries torn asunder, books used for kindling, and art objects stolen or abused, as symbolic domination of others or as punishment for dissent against the approved religious or political beliefs of the conquerors.

From the Roman defeat of Carthage, through Hitler's public burning of books he found inimical to National Socialism, to today's censorship of various types, war, whether violent or political, has been the enemy of books. And the new electronic communications media are subject to the same negative effects. The literature of information science already contains examples of attempts to censor electronic databases or to keep the information they contain out of the possession of persons or nations whose economic interests or political aims threaten one's own. Transborder flow of information is seen to be of potentially equal destructive power as was outright theft of chained books in medieval libraries, and with good reason. Huge amounts of money or power stand to be lost (and gained) through electronic surveillance or illegal theft or copying of sensitive or proprietary information. The implications for information professionals are staggering.

NATIONAL LIBRARIES

Once people began identifying themselves with nation-states, whether based on common geography, common language, or common goals, it was only a matter of time until their literatures were seen as national treasures and the job of collecting and preserving those treasures was assigned to a central authority. This is the wellspring of national libraries, beginning with la Bibliothèque Nationale, Paris (dating from 1622) and followed by the Preussische Staatsbibliothek in Berlin (1659), the Kongelige Bibliothek (Danish National Library) in Copenhagen (1661), La Biblioteca Nacional in Madrid (1712), and La Biblioteca Nazionale in Florence (1727; later renamed la Biblioteca Nazionale Centrale).

In 1759, the British Museum became a de facto national library, and in 1796 the Biblioteca Nacional de Portugal was founded at Lisbon. The Nederlandische Staatsbibliotheek was founded in The Hague in the same year, and in 1800 President Thomas Jefferson founded the Library of Congress in Washington, D.C., and appointed the first Librarian of Congress, John James Beckley. In laying out his ideas for the library, Jefferson wrote that there should be no books of entertainment and no foreign books. "I have confined the catalogue to those branches of science which belong to the deliberations of the members as statesmen."[3] (The Library of Congress is discussed further in chapter 4.)

PHILANTHROPY

A major factor in the proliferation of public libraries in the West was the philanthropic largesse of Andrew Carnegie (1835-1919), who emigrated as a young man from Scotland to the United States and quickly made a huge fortune in iron and steel. Carnegie attributed his great success to hard work and thrift, but even more to the fact that he could and did read widely. He attributed the superior quality of his firm's steel to the fact that he had read up on his subject, replicated the experiments of Bessemer and other European steelmakers, and devised ways to improve upon them. To him, this proved the virtue of reading.

Later, when he was seeking a vehicle for philanthropy, he decided upon libraries, which had given him the knowledge and techniques he needed to get rich. As a way of sharing his good fortune and encouraging others to emulate his example, he made the offer that any city in the United States (or in Canada and beyond) whose government would agree to staff and place books in a library building would receive money to pay for the construction of the building. Many cities took Carnegie up on his offer, agreeing to acquire a site, purchase the books, and hire the staff in exchange for a free library building. From 1886 until the early years of this century, Carnegie spent over $45 million in the United States alone and another $15 million abroad. Some of the buildings so built or commissioned are still standing; undeniably, Carnegie's influence shaped the dispersion and proliferation of public libraries throughout the United States, Canada, and numerous other countries.

DOCUMENTATION AND INFORMATION SCIENCE

Information science is very difficult to define. One definition, both cynical and circular, says that information science is that which is done by information scientists, and vice versa. The field of information science, however, may be defined as one that investigates the properties and behavior of information, how it is transferred from one mind to another, and optimal means for making that transfer, in both natural and artificial systems. Finally, information science is concerned with the effects of information on people and on machines.

Documentation was split off from librarianship at the turn of the twentieth century because the amount of printed material had outstripped the ability of conventional, contemporary library methods to keep pace with it. Especially in the sciences, there was so much information around that it was becoming increasingly difficult to control it and to make it retrievable. Indexing and abstracting had been developed decades earlier and classification had been around for centuries, in one form or another, but practitioners of librarianship needed new techniques that could provide a good, solid handle on information and make it retrievable. This process is still called documentation in Britain; in the United States it has come to be known as information science, while Soviet science has taken to calling it informatics.

Librarianship, always an eclectic discipline, borrowed liberally from other fields and areas of study, such as statistics, to accomplish its first halting steps toward documentation, but it was the progress in mechanization during World War II that gave rise to today's information science. The quest was to find techniques to apply scientific principles to previously non-scientific procedures in librarianship. As examples, British scientist S. C. Bradford studied the dispersion of scientific contributions to a given field in the periodical literature in the 1940s. Herman Fussler, an American academic librarian, is given credit for first applying citation analysis to scientists' use of literature in their fields. Derek Price theorized that there is a mathematical ratio between the important documents in a given field of science and the number of people publishing in that field.

Automation greatly facilitated the analysis and prediction of reading and publishing behavior within and among disciplines, as well as efforts to cope with information overload engendered by the "doubling time" of its total volume (now approaching twelve years and dropping fast). Systems theory, beginning and elaborated in other fields, has made possible library networks based on predictive models of user behavior. Intriguing theories, such as one which states that 20 percent of the books in a given library collection will satisfy 80 percent of the demand, challenge the profession to think about just *which* 20 percent is valuable, which has obvious implications for selection criteria and decisions. Cooperative arrangements between and among libraries are based on predictive models of library behavior, and systems theory makes it possible to manipulate groups of disparate agencies for mutual gain.

Documentation didn't just suddenly become information science. The Shannon-Weaver model became the basis of what we now call information theory. Wiener, at about the same time, was working out some studies in "cybernetics," which dealt with the automation of processes previously performed manually, slowly, and repetitively.[4] Federal support for such projects was forthcoming, as governmental agencies realized the potential of such new ideas for making the gathering, storing, and use of information an easier task despite the constantly escalating total amount of that information.

Substituting the computer for human work has been the overriding force in library attempts to adapt or adopt documentation and information science to our field. Few of us are so rash as to predict that computers (even though they continue to grow faster, more powerful, and more reliable) will one day do all the tasks performed by people. There are still several intellectual operations that people will always do better than machines. But science is working on the problem, and in the future ... who knows? As to whether information science is a true scientific discipline and whether it is separate and distinct from librarianship, this is left to the reader to decide. Perhaps the best reason that we are all having so much trouble defining what information science is and what it is supposed to be doing is that the field is fluid and seems to make itself up as it goes along.

Following is a more in-depth discussion of the ways in which documentation and information science have affected libraries and the work of information professionals.

FIFTY YEARS OF SALIENT ISSUES
CONFRONTING INFORMATION PROFESSIONALS

The 1940s and 1950s

Microforms. The advent of microform storage of information allowed dozens of pages of typed or printed information to be stored on a small, relatively indestructible plastic sheet or roll of film. Microforms could be viewed through simple lenses and projected onto a planar surface, assisting both preservation and miniaturization of materials in libraries and information centers. The chief issue related to this technology is getting people to accept and utilize microforms in place of the more convenient, but easily destructible and space-taking paper products. It is also troublesome that copying microform pages normally involves charges for the consumer.

Dissemination of Information. Dissemination of scientific and technical information began with the recognition that information shared could do much to accelerate improvement of the collective lot of humankind. Modern methods of transmission, together with the realization that information could be given away, sold, or shared but still retained, created a focus on this critical aspect of information transfer. An important issue was and is that dissemination of information is frequently hampered, not unexpectedly, by possessiveness, greed, suspicion, and international tensions and conflict.

Computers. Computers were large, slow, erratic, and terrifically expensive at first. Still, even prototype models demonstrated that it was possible to use machine applications to input, store, process, and generate information, as well as to perform the "numbers crunching" calculations for which automated systems were originally designed. There have been myriad issues related to computers over the years, but perhaps the most salient is that the expensive new technology has served to exacerbate the already-widening gap between society's "haves" and "have-nots." The computer also has made it possible to assemble electronic dossiers on private citizens, rendering surveillance easier than ever before, with potentially chilling consequences.

Machine Translation. Early attempts at accurate machine translation from language to language were either comical or dismal failures, but fifty years of subsequent efforts have produced strides in this area. Still, as one example, much remains to be solved in the problems attendant upon converting colloquial, standard written English into analogous teminology in other tongues or vice versa. The obvious issue with machine translation is the risk of mistranslation, leading to misinterpretation and misunderstanding, which may have ruinous international or economic consequences.

Coordinate Indexing. It was always the dream of information professionals to find a reliable and simple way to ask for two subjects at the same time. An information system that can retrieve this *and* that is vastly superior to one that can only handle one subject at a time. The expanding power of computers and the rules of Boolean logic applied to machine capabilities made it possible, for the first time, to search a large body of documents for two or more concepts simultaneously. The issue with coordinate indexing is one which anyone who has used computers can name: computers do not do what you *want* them to do, they do precisely what you *tell* them to do. The results of literal understanding of human intentions may be amusing or disastrous, but they are often far from what was desired or intended.

Scientific Documentation. The immediate antecedent of what we now call information science was a developing series of theoretical and practical rules that permitted tracing the flow of written communication in general and information transfer in particular. The issue with all such attempts to apply rules to human behavior is that information flow, among other topics, does not always follow rules, creating cognitive dissonance in people and machines alike.

Data Processing. The idea of coded and punched cards as vehicles for instructing and programming computers to follow instructions dates back over a century. Data processing made it possible to create elaborate programs and data sets, which, when fed to computers, would execute thousands, even millions, of instructions in a comparatively short time. One issue concerned with punch-card data processing was that there was no margin for error. Every instruction had to be in its place, which led to numerous frustrating failures for programs that were unable to run correctly. These failures often led to costs, delays, and frustration, as computers of those times were unable to move beyond the limitations of the input they were given.

Xerography. This term refers to the ability to reproduce documents quickly, inexpensively, with high resolution, and in desired (and limitless) quantities. Named for Xerox, the impact of xerography on both the photocopying industry and information transfer is immeasurable. Perhaps the thorniest issue to come out of this development is that reproduction of paper pages is so easy and so widespread that anyone can do it, leading to constant and costly copyright violations, for which corporations and governments have not been able to come up with a solution.

The 1960s

Citation Indexing. Every term in an entry is a potential access point, and the ability to make data entry to a file and retrieve individual records in all kinds of ways has vastly improved upon traditional forms of access to information. One issue concerning this science is that persons of inadequate skill or forethought are involved in marking and parking documents in automated systems, while the rest of us confront the task of trying to access those documents using our own understanding of terms and meanings. A related issue is sometimes called "inter-indexer inconsistency," meaning that, as people do not think alike, they are bound to make varying judgments as to what any document is really about.

Selective Dissemination of Information. SDI creates for each user of a system a profile of desired or needed topics. A computer program quickly examines and "kicks out" all documents that conform to that stored profile. This serves the important purpose of routing information to those who need it most at their workstations, in desired amounts, while those for whom it is judged valueless need not be bothered with it or even know about it. Among issues concerning SDI are the intensive labor and concomitant costs of setting up and maintaining such a system and the obvious fact that such systems cannot, even now, be said to be without bugs, even though they improve all the time.

User Needs. For the first time, close scrutiny of the needs of information users was undertaken during this period. A pleasant development was the discovery that computers were extremely useful tools for ascertaining and keeping handy information on the needs of computer users. Among the problems here is that people do not always have the ability to articulate their needs, while both information professionals and their automated systems must work with what they are given, not always what they truly need.

Information Flow. The venerated Shannon-Weaver model of information transfer and feedback (popularly represented as *who* says *what* to *whom* through *which* channel, with *what* effect?) was subjected to a series of refinements that made it possible to study and predict optimal ways of moving and sharing information. The most serious problem with all studies of information flow to date is that generalization from samples, however reliable the technique in research methodology, cannot account for all members of a group and their information needs.

Information Analysis Centers. These centers were established to focus on the content of information to extract clues about past, present, and future behavior and conditions. Applications of information analysis vary from weather prediction to a host of agricultural uses, to attempts to predict terrorist activities, tracking their movements and published threats. Other systems have been set up to acquire, organize, store, collate, and disseminate information. Among these were such large United States operations as the National Technical Information System (NTIS) and the Educational Resources Information Clearinghouse (ERIC), huge government-sponsored clearinghouses which do their best to amass available information on scientific and educational matters and organize that information into machine-readable databases for public use. Among critical issues related to such centers is the trend to privatize them, transferring them from tax-supported, government utilities to for-profit corporations. As a result, most of the nation's citizens are financially unable to access the information these computers contain.

Pattern Recognition. The general principle by which information is retrieved from electronic databases is pattern recognition. A user with a specific information need must fashion a query such that the system will recognize the symbols used in the typed query and match them to the terms stored in the database of records, retrieving only the ones with patterns shared between the database and the query. A significant issue in pattern recognition has to do with artificial intelligence, which would direct and focus the terminology of the user into terms recognizable by the electronic system.

Thesauri. In the electronic sense, thesauri are lists of approved or authorized terms available to the user of a system for construction of clear, acceptable, and unambiguous search queries. These have rendered the job of consulting machine files less difficult by facilitating pattern matching. Online thesauri, available on some databases, sometimes translate inadmissible terminology into terms the program can understand and respond to. One issue involving thesaurus construction deals with the loss of freedom afforded by free-text searching, in which the user selects the terminology to be employed in the search process.

Computer Typesetting. Small press and personal publication was given a tremendous boost by computer typesetting. It was no longer necessary to own a printing press or to settle for photocopied typed pages in order to publish one's own information. Computer typesetting gave users the ability to create, correct, and print out their own publications, saving much time and expense. Perhaps the principal issue in computer typesetting is that publishers and printers, now frequently bypassed in the publishing process and lacking any government subsidies, are encountering economic difficulties as a result of the amateur publishing going on. Another major issue is that self-published material is not subjected to outside scrutiny and is therefore often lacking in quality and/or accuracy.

The 1970s

Minicomputers. In the 1940s, one walked *into* the computer, not just over to it. Such prototype computers required constant cooling and maintenance and had extremely limited memory and ability. Minicomputers reduced computing to smaller machines not much larger than a two-drawer filing cabinet, but with vastly augmented ability. Computers had grown much more powerful, capable, and less expensive, which brought automation to a range of office and library and information applications that were previously done either laboriously and manually or by large, space-consuming, budget-busting mainframes. Two important issues of minicomputers were that they were still beyond the means of most people who could use them and that they were frequently misused by people who didn't understand how they work.

Online Databases. Large commercial online databases, such as DIALOG and BRS, became available to the commercial, academic, and personal user in the early 1970s, an outgrowth of our nation's defense department's need for rapid, precise information. Through them, by means of a handful of simple, English-language commands, it became possible for a user to search dozens of electronic files efficiently without leaving the room. The downside of this capability was price. Most electronic files cost upwards of $50 an hour to search, with telecommunications costs extra. It became possible, through thorough knowledge of the system and elaborate preparation, to perform a comprehensive and productive search of a file or several files in a matter of minutes.

Networks. Computers were linked by telecommunications so that the user at any terminal of the system could communicate with any other terminal, either directly or via a central system node. Direct communication afforded the user instant access to the information stored within the computer, but telecommunications hook-ups made it possible for one's computer, acting as a terminal, to interface with virtually any other computer equipped with similar equipment.

Word Processing. The abilities to create a document on one's computer, store it, modify it, print it, carry it away on disk, add to it, delete from it, and reprint it have revolutionized the authoring of all types of documents, from letters to term papers to best-sellers. The advantages of using word processing over conventional typing for manuscript preparation and production are too numerous and too obvious to mention.

Transborder Data Flow. After all the glowing praise for this new technology, there are a host of concerns. Harking back to the remarkable property of information that it can be shared without loss to the original owner, the question arises: Does information become less valuable when more people are in possession of it? International espionage does not merely refer to surveillance of other nations' activities. It can now take place when one nation deliberately steals or appropriates the information of another. A large number of incidents of this nature have awakened information-rich nations like the United States to the various problems arising from the ability of others (e.g., Iraq) to capture, and appropriate to themselves, private or sensitive information, without permission or compensation.

Freedom of Information. This is a shared desire and belief inherent in the American way of democracy. Yet if all information were to be free to all who desired it, without restrictions of any kind, another problem would be created. This problem is actually a large number of problems, bearing the collective name *privacy* issues.

Privacy. Another privilege of a free society, which most of its citizens consider a right, is privacy. Yet the right to privacy often and strongly clashes with the *freedom of information* we hold so dear. Extremely important issues, such as freedom of information and privacy of records and the ways in which these contradict each other, are discussed at greater length in chapters 9 and 10.

Fee-Based Services. A capitalist, free-market society like our Western civilization leads to the systemization of profit and loss. Information, having demonstrable value in economic terms, is not given away or shared under normal circumstances. It is sold. And the sale of information and information services creates a strong barrier to people's abilities to improve their lives through the acquisition of important, useful information. The ever-present gap between society's "haves" and "have-nots" is only aggravated when information is sold to those who can afford it, rather than made available to those who truly need it regardless of ability to pay. This issue, perhaps more than any other we face, threatens to divide the information community and will resurface in several other parts of this book.

The 1980s

Personal Computers. PCs have done for the ordinary person's ability to create, modify, and produce documents just about what, over 500 years ago, Gutenberg's printing press did for the ability to buy, own, sell, and even write books. It is no exaggeration to suggest that the relatively inexpensive PC has completely changed the lives of most people, changing those lives so completely that to return to old ways of writing seems primitive and annoying. Even though there are still many persons who are resistant to the idea of using computers for any purpose, their numbers are fewer and fewer all the time, as new generations of schoolchildren are growing up screen- and keyboard-oriented. The objection that computers are often prone to error, leading to costly, sometimes devastating, mistakes, cannot be swept aside as trivial. It is, however demonstrable that refinements in operating systems and improved familiarity of computer operators with their software systems have combined to lessen the frequency and severity of these problems.

Librarians and other information professionals have jumped on the PC bandwagon in a big way. The number of applications programs available to libraries that can run on existing hardware continues to grow, so that almost any library can afford some sort of PC system for internal record-keeping at least, if not for public use. Steadily improving technology has resulted in price breaks. One issue connected with the proliferation of PCs is that of compatibility, meaning that there is little standardization of computers and many of them are still incapable of talking to each other.

Video. Another development of the last decade that has revolutionized our libraries is video. Libraries had generally stocked films for various uses (entertainment, instruction, self-help) by the general public. However, these were reel-to-reel, easily damaged or distorted, and required expensive projectors for their use. The advent of the videocassette recorder/player (VCR) has permitted libraries of all types to acquire (at reasonable cost), store, and circulate videos in convenient, easy-to-use formats with minimal potential for damage.

Video development has raised other questions, concerning such matters as copyright and content suitability. What remedy is there for the producer or distributor if any citizen with a VCR is capable of copying a program and using it for any desired purpose, without compensation to or even notification of the owner. Additionally, there is no evidence concerning the effect of watching videocassettes in the privacy of one's home on young people, a subject in need of more investigation. The convenience of the format, together with the comparatively low cost and availability of the equipment necessary for its use, has changed forever the notion that libraries are places where one only gets books.

CD-ROM. Compact disk-read only memory, literally a database on a disk, has permitted libraries to offer access to large-scale files of machine-readable information without telecommunications costs or fear of destruction of information. While the acquisition of CD-ROM disks and players represents a considerable initial expense for the library, once the initial purchases are made the library can offer electronic access to information virtually cost-free, with minimal further outlay.

The principal downside of CD-ROM technology is that each CD-ROM disk is like a snapshot, in that it represents things as they are at the moment of creation, rather than an ongoing accretion of information. CD-ROM disks available to libraries and information centers cannot be altered or modified, and the library, as purchaser, can only keep current by subscribing to periodic updates or by purchasing new editions. Thus, while CD-ROM has, in part, freed libraries from having to worry about the frequently ruinous costs of commercial online database searching, it is generally not the equivalent of actual interactive searching and is at best only a partial solution to patrons' information needs. Many CD-ROM products now offer a linkage to commercial online databases, so that searches can be constructed off-line, then sent over telephone lines to databases when they are deemed correct, a very cost-effective method.

Artificial Intelligence. AI represents a triumph of the new technology. It has improved rapidly in recent years. Expert systems and improved computer capabilities have created machines that not only perform complex tasks (e.g., diagnosis of medical problems, troubleshooting engines, playing expert chess), but also are capable of learning from their experiences and mistakes and improving their performances, emulating the highest human awareness, if not necessarily tradition. Admittedly, the technology is still young and developing, and obviously such systems are beyond the financial means of most libraries, but artificial intelligence is a hopeful sign for the effective and improving handling of information and materials requests. It may make the job of the information professional much easier and more rewarding in the near future.

Robotics. Robotics, the science of making artificial intelligence mobile and even ambulatory, is one step further along the path to improving the job of library/information provision. Time will permit experimentation with robots, as will analysis of numerous fictional speculative works concerning the development, learning, proliferation, functions, and, inevitably, the problems and hazards of such new creatures. One of the most critical problems of the modern world is that, just because it is possible to do something does not necessarily mean it is desirable to do so. Clearly, the technology of artificial intelligence and robotics will bear watching. There is much to be gained in going ahead with experiments in robotics, but other potential concerns must be addressed as well.[5]

Desktop Publishing. This is a computer development of recent years, whereby computers of sufficient memory and capabilities, using inexpensive software, are enabled to produce and publish professional-looking publications, complete with artwork, photographs, and eye-catching design. This trend is one of the few mostly positive features of the computer revolution, and, if it continues into the future, it will do much to enhance the library's standing with its community. Virtually limitless numbers and types of communications can be created and distributed, with creativity the only limit to the library's capabilities in getting its message across to its public.

Facsimile Transmission. FAXing has been around for a long time, but the closing years of the 1980s saw breakthroughs that permitted libraries to cut communication time to zero, as messages could be sent and received easily from place to place as quickly as telephone lines could encode digitized signals and send them across vast distances (distance, in this context, is technically irrelevant) as acoustic tones, to be reassembled into coherent messages at the other end. The advantages of a reliable, inexpensive, and quasi-universal FAX network so outweigh the costs as to make such machines necessities for libraries, which must constantly interact with other institutions. Along with FAX comes a series of options such as *electronic mail* and *computer conferencing*, which permit library staff members to avoid the costs and problems of travel and time away from the desk in order to "meet" with others for mutual problem-solving. These innovations are not only cost-effective, they also may be seen as environmentally sound, since virtually any form of travel nowadays consumes non-renewable resources.

Downloading. The capability of a library to capture information transmitted by telephone to a terminal, store it on disk, and work with it subsequent to severing telephonic communication is yet another great stride forward in facilitating the information professional's job. Downloading, however, in the absence of a strong code and sense of what our profession has come to call *information ethics,* can lead to abuses, lawsuits, and restrictions on privileges. The problems subsumed under information ethics are so important to the profession that they are discussed in greater detail in chapter 10.

History flows like a river, and anyone who stops to review the past, even the immediate past, has merely chosen a place to stand from which to survey the current of events. This chapter has reviewed only some of the recent developments in library and information provision that affect the information profession's ability to serve its clients. Despite recent arguments to the contrary, history really has no middle and no end. Imagination, technology, and constraints, as they always have, will combine to facilitate or impede the library in carrying out its mission, goals, and objectives.

NOTES

[1] Alvin Toffler. *Future Shock* (New York: Random House, 1970).

[2] Marshall McLuhan. *Understanding Media: The Extensions of Man* (New York: McGraw-Hill, 1964).

[3] Thomas Jefferson. *Writings*, ed. by Merrill P. Peterson (New York: Literary Classics of the United States, 1984), p. 1354.

[4] Norbert Wiener. *Cybernetics: Control and Communication in the Animal and the Machine* (New York: John Wiley, 1948).

[5] Bruce A. Shuman. *The Library of the Future: Alternative Scenarios for Information Professionals* (Englewood, Colo.: Libraries Unlimited, Inc., 1989). One scenario involves the interaction of a naive patron and a programmed "reference robot" in a future public library. Isaac Asimov's *I, Robot* (Garden City, New York: Doubleday, 1963), a work of science fiction, cleverly explains through fictional narrative what some of the problems with programming artificial intelligence might be. Imagine, if you dare, that the mind of a robot is equally susceptible to madness and violence as are human minds, and the potential for tragedy should be obvious.

REFERENCE LIST

Butler, Pierce. *An Introduction to Library Science.* Chicago: University of Chicago Press, 1933; reprint, 1961.

Harris, Michael H. *History of Libraries in the Western World.* Metuchen, N.J.: Scarecrow Press, 1984.

_____. "The Purpose of the American Public Library: A Revisionist Interpretation of History." *Library Journal* (September 15, 1973): 2509-14.

Jackson, Sidney L. *Libraries and Librarianship in the West: A Brief History.* New York: McGraw-Hill, 1974.

McLuhan, Marshall. *Understanding Media: The Extensions of Man.* New York: New American Library, 1984.

Rayward, W. Boyd. "Library and Information Science: An Historical Perspective." *Journal of Library History* 20 (1985): 120-36.

Rogers, A. R., and Kathryn McChesney. *The Library in Society.* Littleton, Colo.: Libraries Unlimited, 1984.

Shera, Jesse H. "Causal Factors in Public Library Development." In *Reader in American Library History*, edited by Michael H. Harris, 141-62. Washington, D.C.: National Cash Register, 1971.

_____. *Introduction to Library Science.* Littleton, Colo.: Libraries Unlimited, 1976.

_____. *Sociological Foundations of Librarianship.* New York: Asia Publishing House, 1970.

Wiegand, Wayne A. "The Role of the Library in American History." In *Bowker Annual.* 33d ed., 69-76. New York: R. R. Bowker, 1988.

3

General Issues for Libraries and Information Centers

THE PROLIFERATION OF INFORMATION

Before considering the particular problems of the different types of libraries and information centers, it is important to explain why they are needed now more than ever. It is estimated that more information has been produced in the last 30 years than in the previous 5,000. Moreover, the total amount of information has doubled and is expected to keep doubling every twelve to fourteen years. This means that if the total amount of information in existence in 1940 was X, using the twelve-year doubling rule we estimate that the total was 2X in 1952, 4X by 1964, 8X by 1976, 16X by the year 1988, and will top out at about 32X by the turn of the century.

To cope with this relentless doubling of information and to make sense of its complexity so that one may reliably find appropriate needles in enormous haystacks, skilled information specialists are increasingly going to be needed who possess the skill and ability to find desired information and to exploit it to the fullest.

FUNCTIONS OF THE LIBRARY IN SOCIETY

Even though the library is frequently defined not so much by what it is as what it does, discussed here are the general functions of the library.

The Educational Function

Clearly, academic and school libraries are educational, both in function and in services (as is discussed further in chapter 7). The public library has a more traditional function of providing informal education through provision of materials that assist individuals in learning, self-improvement, and generally managing their lives. Years ago, when societal and economic factors frequently forced individuals out of the school system at a very early age, the public library became "the people's university," where citizens no longer in school could continue their studies on their own time, on subjects of their own choosing, and at their own pace. The public library often works together with the community school system to provide enrichment materials for students beyond those offered by school libraries. In some communities, in fact, the school system and the public library system are jointly operated and funded, although opinion is frequently divided as to whether such arrangements prove to be mutually beneficial to those agencies.

The Archival Function

The first, and perhaps the most frequently cited, task of libraries was and is the physical preservation (and sometimes restoration) of the graphic record. The term *graphic record* is used here to denote anything recorded, whether on stone, clay, paper, canvas, magnetized surfaces, etc., which can be "read" by others. All academic libraries and most public libraries preserve, maintain, and sometimes restore written records for the benefit of a rather poorly defined concept known collectively as *posterity*.

The library, in performing this function, is acting out humanity's desire to have a link with the past and to leave "footprints in the sands of time," with at least some achievements of people's lives noted when they are gone. Most libraries carry out their archival function by collecting materials, storing them under optimal conditions, and making them available so that they may be used or consulted by future generations of society.

The Recreational Function

Academic and school libraries have as their primary mission support for the educational curriculum of the institution. This does not release the academic or school library from the necessity of providing recreational library materials, but it does place recreation in a secondary role. The public library, however, may proclaim that it exists to satisfy the information and entertainment needs of the citizens of the community, but many people look upon it primarily as a place to use or borrow books and other materials for recreational purposes. Some public librarians express dismay that many members of the public not only do not avail themselves of the informational and other services of public libraries, but are unaware that such services exist. Still it is fair to say that only the public library places recreational ends high in its list of service priorities.

Such a role may be justified easily. Consider this economic argument: The public library can, through the purchase of a single copy of a book, satisfy the desire to read it for a theoretically limitless number of readers, assuming that they wait patiently for it and that the physical book stands up to the rigors of typical circulation and wear. Societally, this casts the public library in a collective role, as it is able, by spending a comparatively small amount of money, to render unnecessary the need for each reader of a given book to spend money on the item.

The question is: Which materials, among competing and equally available ones, should the library buy? There are essentially two competing schools of thought on this issue, which we shall call, for convenience, the demand principle and the prescription principle. (Adherents actually cover a continuum rather than espousing discrete alternatives.)

Simply stated, the demand principle maintains that it is the legitimate role of the library (especially the public library) to attempt to ascertain what people *want* to read (or hear or view), and then provide it to them, given the limits of funding and the understanding that the materials provided are intended to satisfy the needs of the *entire* community as much as possible.

By contrast, the prescription principle decrees that it is both obvious and important to realize that some materials are "better" than others and that purchasing the better ones will have a better effect on the audience for which they are purchased. Following this logic, librarians (with recommendations, both formal and informal, from community members) are charged with the responsibility of selecting those *materials that will do somebody some good* (however *good* is defined) and, at the same time, of avoiding the rest.

Prescription principle adherents believe, for whatever reasons they care to elaborate, that the following propositions are true:

1. Not all materials available to libraries are good, useful, helpful, or worthwhile for people to spend (waste?) their time on.

2. Materials that are none of the above may be called, for want of better terminology, *junk*.

3. Avoid buying junk. Money is in short supply and junk is readily available elsewhere (in bookstores, drugstores, airports, etc.).

4. Because junk is frequently attractive because of content, seductive advertising, human weakness, or pretty packaging, someone has to have the intelligence and resistance to temptation to be able to sort out the junk from the quality merchandise.

5. That someone might as well be the librarian, who is expected to have at least some mix of inbred discrimination and educational course-work that makes junk easier to identify and avoid than it would be for the layperson to do.

6. Even though people frequently like, and will request, junk, it is the duty of the librarian not to pander to their base or futile tastes, and instead to buy quality books and other materials. That this argument flies in the face of the demand principle is obvious. But then again, say the "prescriptionists," so what? Most libraries have worked out some method of compromise, whereby they do their level best to satisfy the recreational demands of their public and still set aside some of the budget for the purchase of "classics" and works deemed important.

As is true of all library-related issues, there is more than one valid viewpoint about these matters. Be honest! Don't you have your own list of materials that you regard as *junk*? Or dangerous in the wrong hands? Or unsafe for children? Or simply vile, disgusting, and repugnant? Of course you do. But the Library Bill of Rights is unequivocal on this point:

Books and other library resources should be provided for the interest, information, and enlightenment of all people in the community the library serves. Materials should not be excluded because of the origin, background, or views of those contributing to their creation.[1]

This statement would appear to encompass, among other rights, the right to find one's own tastes, whatever they may be, reflected in library materials.

The Social Function

Social interaction is among the strongest of normal human needs. The library, regardless of type, is frequently viewed as a social place, where one may encounter other users in the library's audience or community by chance or by prearrangement. Sometimes this freedom of interaction can get out of hand. Often, in academic and public libraries, it appears that most of the building's public rooms (and sometimes restrooms) have been taken over by people who have come not in search of library materials or information, but only to meet others, for a variety of purposes. Libraries normally do not encourage use for exclusively non-bibliothecal purposes. But the days of the severe older librarian (see "Images of the Librarian/Information Professional" in chapter 1) with finger firmly pressed to lips, going around "shushing" people are, we hope, behind us.

Most modern libraries allow a certain degree of latitude to talkers and socializers. Librarians generally consider it important to attempt to create a warm, comfortable environment where patrons can, within limits, do what they want. One doesn't have to talk to anyone, or explain the purpose of the visit, or bring money or show serious intention, in order to be permitted to remain in the building. And if such laxity of admission criteria means that the homeless, the deranged, and the loitering frequent our buildings, it can't be helped; that's why we hire security guards.

Generally, except in the case of certain manifestations of problem patron behavior, the public or academic library tends to encourage social interaction, and by so doing, to be part of community life.

The Uplift Function

Since early colonial days in America, religious leaders and reformers have preached against the perils of idle hands. Libraries of all types were welcomed by reformers as places where one could spend leisure hours reading materials that would serve to uplift spirits and thus bring the mind (and body) nearer to one's God. Library leaders, in combination with religious ones, urged that libraries become viable alternatives to such wasteful, and often sinful, leisure-time pursuits as the saloon, the brothel, and the gaming parlour.

Libraries, then, were seen as potentially positive forces in uplifting and reforming minds and spirits, especially those of the young and impressionable, provided that the contents of those libraries were beyond reproach, containing material suitable for developing religious faith and encouraging young people to resist or shun temptation and sin. To a certain extent, this concept still influences many library policies, especially in parochial schools and academic institutions and in public libraries in rural areas and smaller communities. Today, many clergy still enthusiastically preach the value of reading approved materials as a supplemental uplift mechanism to prayer, with the stakes in the game being the eventual disposition of one's everlasting soul. Along with such emphasis, naturally, comes censorship, which is why public libraries have to a large extent outgrown this reformist movement in favor of a more libertarian approach to materials selection.

The Utilitarian Function

The next time you're in the library, go over to the card catalog or an online terminal and search for materials whose titles begin with the words "How to...." Larger online union catalogs may have well over 5,000 monographic title entries beginning with this heading. High school and college libraries frequently gather such books together into vocational collections for the use of students seeking career planning assistance, and public libraries supply great numbers of "how-to" books for the self-improvement needs of users. This wealth of material, designed to serve as self-instruction for people who want to acquire new skills, demonstrates the library's commitment to making available works that can teach new things.

How to live on practically nothing ... How to build a birdhouse ... How to make your marriage, or other relationship, work ... How to score high on the College Entrance Examination ... How to play chess ... How to write your own unbreakable will and save a bundle on lawyer's fees ... How to watch professional football .... These are but a few of the library materials to be found under this title or in a separate self-improvement section. They serve as evidence that the utilitarian principle, which says that libraries have a mission of providing information and materials that will assist citizens and users with the know-how they require to lead fuller, better, or more constructive lives, is alive and well.

The Study Hall Function

While it is true that a satisfying modern life involves encounters with people, many of us, in order to find solitude, consolation, privacy, or a comfortable environment for study and intense concentration, welcome the library as a place where we can just sit down and think. Large numbers of students, who live in homes where they are bombarded by the sounds and noises of others, seek out the school or public library as a place where no one hassles them, so they can attempt to get in a few hours of uninterrupted contemplation and thought.

Libraries, however, must juggle competing demands, and it is not always possible for patrons to find a cozy, quiet corner for study or contemplation. That is one of the reasons that libraries have circulating materials. It is possible in most libraries for people to remove the books and other materials from the noisy, often crowded precincts of the building and to carry them to a park bench, a rowboat, their beds, or some other place where they can concentrate. Within the walls of the building, however, the library provides, as best it can, an array of study facilities, with reference materials present for consultation. However, problems arise because those who wish to discuss, debate, laugh aloud, and even dispute are at odds with those who need quiet. In some cases this situation is easily remedied through a partition of facilities, but most libraries are restricted in available space and remodeling funding and find that they cannot oblige those who need a quiet place to study *and* those who need a busy place to conduct their daily affairs.

The Research Center Function

Research, according to the dictionary, refers to a systematic inquiry into a subject in order to discover or check facts. But it is much, much more. Research can be said to be an attempt to push back the boundaries of the unknown and enhance the domain of what we know about our world and how best to live within it or on it (or even apart from it). Research may be said to occur when a man under a tree observes an apple's fall and draws conclusions about natural phenomena. Research also takes place when investigation into the work of others leads one to hypotheses or conclusions that extend or alter the others' work. And research, while it doesn't necessarily require anything in the way of tools, normally operates optimally when the researcher is surrounded by, or has easy access to, a very large body of stored information, for checking facts and for defining what is known before trying to move on into new territory.

Most modern research that does not take place in the empirical (scientific) area and that does not require the use of a laboratory for experimentation is greatly enhanced by the presence of a major research library. It is the function of the research library to acquire materials in many areas, in considerable depth, to organize them for easy use, and to make them available to the right people at the right time in amounts commensurate with their needs. The research function of the library dictates that a collection of materials is available for users to consult to establish a base for original and creative thought in the large and shadowy area of that which is not yet known. To facilitate such inquiry, the library (and its personnel) assists the research function by providing materials, workspace, facilities, and services, as needed.

The Activist/Advocate/Change-Agent Function

Increasingly, in recent years, some librarians have urged that it should be a function of the library and information center not only to mirror and reflect popular tastes and societal values, but to take an active role in changing them for the better. The obvious question becomes then *what* is better, and better for whom? Under this activist philosophical banner, the library's employees do not sit idly by, selecting materials and providing services under the demand principle, but instead seek to make positive changes in the popular consciousness through raising that consciousness to higher levels. An interesting casualty of this belief system is the time-honored notion (endorsed by the American Library Association among others) that a library must purchase and display materials and information on all sides of any issue. In this way, librarians join forces with those who feel that some materials and services are *better* for most individuals, and for society as a whole, than are others, and that it is the mission and duty of the library to emphasize positive values and role models, while de-emphasizing stereotypes and negative, discarded, or false values and role models. By way of example, suppose a library staff, citing its mission to elevate the popular consciousness, refused to acquire and make available works that were racist, sexist, anti-semitic, or pornographic? The result might be a "cleansing" of the content of the library, but at what cost? Clearly, the price of attempting to be "politically correct" is the suppression of freedom of speech, regardless of the motivations of those taking the action. Just suppose that library directors, feeling that their personal views and attitudes are of sufficient value to outweigh democratic information provision, decide to provide material on only one side of such difficult issues as abortion, capital punishment, vegetarianism, or the Middle East peace process.

Two problems arise with the noble and lofty goal of improving popular attitudes and ideas. The first problem is that there is no concerted opinion on just which materials will produce desirable social results (which calls for strict definition), and, perhaps more important, we all cannot truly hope to agree on just which results are most desirable. Additionally, if one looks carefully, one may see actions designed to bring about desirable change as acts of censorship and repression, which are certainly inconsistent with the ideals and institutions of a democratic society. How, for example, can the library subscribe to the notion that users ought to be able to find what they want in the collection of materials and, at the same time, change (and raise) people's consciousness on the sensitive and controversial issues of the day? Perhaps more important, *should* libraries attempt this?

When librarians elect to become change-agents, they unavoidably shift, philosophically, from the studied neutrality they have striven to maintain into the treacherous waters of social advocacy, which earns them enemies as well as friends. Is this desirable? Does taking positions on social issues place a library on a collision course with disaster? Is it political suicide to espouse one cause (say, one political party's platform) over another? Should librarians remain passive and mute on the important issues of the day? Is it possible that silent librarians may forfeit their institutions and their jobs because they failed to speak out on social issues, while they still had voices and audiences? Finally, are we, as information professionals, bound to articulate only the values of our institutions, or are we morally obliged to voice our own concerns? Librarians, as individuals, can advocate change, but not when they are perceived as speaking for their libraries.

The Information Dissemination Function

Many in the library profession believe that the highest calling of any library or information center is that of information provider, giving users the facts and information they need to conduct their lives as meaningfully and successfully as possible. If this is true, libraries' most important service is dispensing knowledge, data, facts, and reports to people who need them most.✓

Today's large libraries have information and materials on just about any subject, but not all community members are aware that the library is a place where information on virtually all subjects is available, usually free of direct cost, to anyone who asks for it or is eligible to receive it. All librarians have had the experience of meeting people, even those holding high-status, well-paid positions in their communities, who know as little of what libraries have or can do as they do about quantum physics. Frequently, there is some mis-understanding concerning how one gets this information and whether it is available to all equally, or to some more plentifully or readily than to others.

Consider, for example, the case of students. School students have (or should have) libraries provided for their informational and curriculum needs. But schools tend to close early and homework is often done during evening hours. While information provision in public libraries, which normally are open evenings, is generally made to all adults, without regard to race, color, creed, or lifestyle, young persons who identify themselves as students are sometimes given minimal or no assistance in finding what they want. The motivation of the librarian is frequently a shared belief with teachers that people learn best by finding things for themselves, but if that means that — ∳ students are given short shrift and generally treated as second-class citizens, is that fitting and proper? When librarians provide insufficient information for students to find what they want, is that fair? If it is a function of the library to provide information of varying degrees of complexity, in various packaging containers, and at various places, is it right for a library to deny or restrict information provision to one class of users?

The Propaganda Dissemination Function

Finally, and may it never come to this, the public or academic library of today, which champions and espouses no causes, favors no party, and prefers no political philosophy, may, if enough people do nothing to prevent it, be taken over or exploited by governments or by ruling families or pressure groups approved by the dominant powers and used as a disseminator of state-sponsored and state-approved propaganda. It is the mission and purpose of the library (regardless of type) in some totalitarian nations to support the policies and aims of government, with little or no regard for the truth or equality. If one suspends the democratic notion that everyone may expect to be granted automatic admission to the public library without challenge and dismisses as hazardous to the public good the idea that, once inside, one may reasonably expect to find materials on all subjects, written from all points of view, the library becomes a tool of that totalitarianism. Do not assume that it couldn't happen here.

Such conditions occur routinely today in many of the world's nations. It would be possible for this nation to become like those others if faced with a combination of (1) a sense of national emergency; (2) a willingness to rewrite or suspend the Constitution; and (3) library functionaries who, out of patriotism, fear, belief, self-interest, or the understandable need to hold onto their jobs in a recessionary economy, get along by going along with official government policies.

COMMON CHARACTERISTICS OF LIBRARIES AND INFORMATION CENTERS

The following discussion covers the essential characteristics of libraries and information centers, including how they further the missions of their respective institutions.

Materials

The library needs a broad collection of print and non-print materials selected with the specific needs of the users in mind. Such a collection will consist of both English and foreign language materials, depending on the curricular offerings of the academic institution and the expressed or perceived interests and reading abilities of the users of the library. Additionally, hardware and software are needed for access to electronic technologies, including (but not limited to) computers, printers, desktop publishing equipment, digitized imaging, and online searching.

Services

A full-service library will offer its users a vast range of services, not only the traditional ones that are found everywhere, but newer ones, designed to facilitate information-seeking and information-gathering. Examples of these are the inception and development of home-grown databases; file conversion from outmoded systems and classification schemes to more capable, more relevant ones; desktop publishing, which can make virtually any student into an editor/publisher/designer of publications; indexing and abstracting services beyond those commercially available; specialized information centers, where a need is felt to gather, organize, and disseminate information and materials in a highly concentrated subject area; and project management or advice, for grant-seeking and attainment of research goals.

Communications

Integrated facilities, by which is meant a linking of libraries, computer centers, subject departments, and telecommunications facilities, will serve to benefit both in-building and remote users, as networks of computers, FAX machines, telephones, and advanced communications systems (e.g., electronic mail) render distance and travel practically irrelevant in serving the needs of the institution's users.

Innovations

There are some needs that are actually more akin to desires, combining forecasting and wishful thinking. Some of these desires for the library are presently out of the question from a financial standpoint. Others are along the lines of "what we'd do with a generous endowment, a sudden windfall, or a winning lottery ticket." Still others are presently available technologies, simply beyond the means, priorities, or vision of those who shape and direct libraries. Most of these, however (e.g., expert systems, hypertext, interactive instruction, supernetworks) may be just one or two good economic years away and should not be discarded as potential building blocks of the library of the new century.

A few salient issues have always been with us and will very probably remain. Cultural and ethnic diversity may have little effect on the workings of a modern library in a free society, but this issue is bound to influence selection and acquisition policies in the years ahead. Inflation, serving to decrease resources and lessen the purchasing power of the library's dollar, has strong effects on the ability of libraries to make provision for present-day needs and future change.

ISSUES COMMON TO LIBRARIES
AND INFORMATION CENTERS

Personnel Policies

Sometimes the number and types of library staff are imposed upon the library by statutory policy of the school board, academic institution, or city or county government. At other times, a number of assignable positions or a pool of salary and fringe benefit money is assigned to a library system, which has discretion over how many and whom to hire and where to deploy the personnel. This can create a serious barrier to services, as competent and adequate staffing are keys to service provision.

Publisher/Producer Variables

Increasingly, some of the barriers to libraries' ability to acquire and provide the desired materials for their community stem from problems outside the library environment. In addition to rising costs, libraries must often deal with copyright restrictions, licensing agreements, and other rules that prevent the cost-effective provision of information in any library of modest financial means. What is needed is serious thought about the competing interests of publishers, who have reason to expect fair returns on their investments through sales; authors, who justly derive income from royalties and other compensation for their efforts; and libraries, who strive to provide maximum information to their clients, unfettered by legal or ethical problems surrounding ownership and proprietary rights. Such a compromise may not be workable, or even possible, but ongoing efforts are needed to resolve this dilemma.

Security

Security, for materials, for equipment, and for the people who work in and use libraries, is an important issue for discussion. All libraries, whether urban or rural, large or small, general or specialized, need security for the protection of both the variety of costly equipment and materials within the walls and of the people who work in, or use, library facilities. Security comes in various modes and with commensurately varying price tags: staff persons who serve as guards, patrolling the building's corridors and reading rooms as a deterrent to crime, vandalism, and other forms of misbehavior; campus or local police, available when summoned; and electronic or mechanical devices installed in various parts of the building to detect problems. Such items and/or actions as surveillance cameras, anti-theft and anti-tampering devices, fire and burglary alarm systems, bank-style vaults, recording of the serial number of all valuable equipment, locking security doors, and even after-hours patrols are increasingly used by academic libraries to protect their contents.

Another form of library security involves the use of electronic gates and other detection devices designed to prevent patrons from intentionally or unintentionally walking away with the library's materials. Without a doubt, these machines have been successful in deterring or preventing theft, but no such device is of sufficient sophistication that it cannot be defeated by someone seeking to find a way around it. In fact, it has been said that it would take a smart child only a few moments of observation to be able to beat the machine, in one of several ways.

Some types of crime in libraries can be neither predicted nor completely prevented; theft, loss, damage, vandalism, and the like can be made more difficult for the criminal, but can never be stopped.

Access to Library Holdings:
Catalogs – Online, Card, and Book

The traditional library card catalog, featuring range after range and row after row of card catalog cabinets, is rapidly giving way, in almost all large libraries and quite a few of the smaller ones, to automated online catalogs, where the user need only indicate whether an author, title, or subject is desired and then has electronic access to the complete holdings of the host institution's libraries, often integrated into a union catalog with the holdings of other libraries (which may be of different types). Online catalogs thus present enormous advantages over traditional ones: (1) instant access to holdings of several libraries; (2) item availability information; (3) printout capability;

and (4) Boolean search logic (not universally available at the present time), by which two or more concepts may be entered together while linked logically.

There is, however, a corresponding list of drawbacks to the proliferation of online catalogs: (1) persons who have encountered difficulty mastering card catalogs will not necessarily take readily to online ones; (2) browsing, in the sense of leisurely exploration of entries, is difficult or impossible; (3) the number of terminals available governs the number of users who may consult the catalog at the same time; (4) dial-up access from home telephones relieves stress on in-library use, but requires both terminals and modems in the users' homes, and does not solve all the problems of congestion, the need for help, and queuing.

The Preservation Function

Academic libraries, perhaps more than other types, generally recognize their responsibility in the preservation of the graphic record. Responsibility notwithstanding, it is a painfully obvious fact that books and bound period-icals are turning to acid sludge, and, thereafter, to powder, in most libraries, despite our best efforts to control temperature and humidity in the stacks. New treatments will preserve (and sometimes even restore) the condition of printed pages, but such treatments are very expensive and time-consuming beyond the budgets of most libraries. Microfilming projects, once so popular among libraries in the race to preserve and protect their materials, have fallen into dis-favor because, among other things, patrons generally don't enjoy using micro-film and expensive equipment must be purchased to make such materials usable. The debate continues as to the best way(s) of coping with the preserva-tion problem, but academic libraries (and other types, as well) are faced with the very real possibility that books and other reading materials will become in large part unusable and effectively lost by the early years of the next century, unless something is done now to reverse the trend.

Downsizing and Zero-Growth

Many libraries are coping with their budget difficulties by enacting "zero-growth" rules to save space and to keep their collections current. This means that, for each new item accessioned and added to the collection, another item is slated to be weeded or de-accessioned. The eventual disposition of such material varies, with some simply thrown away like trash, after the appro-priate entries are made in the shelflist and catalogs, while others are destroyed, torn apart, consumed by fire, stored, given away, traded, or sold at booksales. This seemingly draconian method of keeping collections at the same size is not as severe or as damaging as it may seem, because a considerable body of research suggests that approximately 80 percent of the requests in any library are accommodated using 20 percent of the collection and that 20 percent tends to be the most recent material. The zero-growth method, therefore, simply suggests that, as newer imprints are added to the collection, older, less current, and obsolete materials are discarded to make room. Of course, age as a criterion of value is a rule that does not necessarily apply in all fields of study. Some of the best books ever written, for example, about French impressionism (both art and music) were written contemporaneously with the artists' lives. An 1892 book on Degas or Manet, therefore, will not be discarded because it is a century old, unless it is in a physical condition that warrants discarding or because better (and newer) publications treat the subject more effectively.

Technical Services

Modern technology has had such a strong impact on the technical aspects of library routines such as acquisition, cataloging, classification, ordering, claiming, accounting, and billing that numerous monographs have been written on the topic. It is not, strictly speaking, within this book's scope to delve into the technical aspects of librarianship, except to note that the changes have been significant (and primarily favorable) and that most academic libraries benefit from automation (although detracting voices may still be heard). The time and labor saved in technical services, however, are demonstrable, and few still dispute that a high-function, integrated technical services department is a boon to any library.

Evaluation

A longstanding problem lies in the complex answer to a simple question: "How good is our library?" This question may be answered in several ways, which may also be expressed as questions. For example, "How well does my library rate when I use these standards or formulae for my type of library?" Or possibly, "How good is my library when I compare it to similar-sized libraries in nearby communities, or colleges or universities in the same geographic area or athletic conference?" Finally, one may ask, "How good do the users of our library say the library is at meeting their informational needs?" This last is probably the best method of all of determining adequacy and merit.

Accountability

Accountability means that the library is expected to account for the money it receives and for the money it spends, using some sort of input and output measures that translate into effectiveness judgments. Accountability also means that the employees of the library are expected to represent their achievements and problems accurately and to be able to defend their decisions to higher administration on the basis of fiscal soundness and relevance to the library's mission. As more and more colleges and universities find that they must run their operations as businesses, rather than as ivory-tower citadels of learning, accountability is a term that will be heard increasingly, with compelling implications for academic libraries.

Unionization

Unionization permits academic librarians to join faculty collective bargaining units seeking to secure better salaries or other working conditions from institutions in which economic conditions are precarious. A problem with this is that some librarians see an inherent ethical conflict between the "service" motivation of libraries and the natural enough desire of employees to augment their wages and secure other benefits of systematized education. The variables here are considerable. In some cases, unionization is not permitted by state law. In other cases, unions are not perceived as necessary because faculty are satisfied with their financial packages and convinced that the administrations have their best interests at heart. But in still other cases, whether or not the academic institution appears to "have" the money to grant adequate increases, the administrations offer paltry (or no) raises and faculty must join together to oppose what they perceive as an unfair distribution of funds. At such times librarians, if they are eligible to join academic unions of faculty (which is quite another question), must choose whether to join the protesters or to go along with whatever terms and conditions are imposed upon them by the administration. The situation really becomes difficult when a strike vote is called and library professionals must choose between "business as usual," which means turning their backs on other faculty members, and "job action," which may seem a dereliction of one's service ethic and could lead to disastrous consequences, from loss of income while the strike continues to dismissal (or other form of official or unofficial punishment) for having joined the rebellious strikers. Collective bargaining is widespread throughout academia these days, and the librarian ought to think carefully about his position on such matters. (Do responsible behavior and professional duty mean that one should grab a picket sign or report to work in the event of a strike?) Clearly, situational and personal variables will determine one's sympathies and one's subsequent behavior, and no generalizations apply.

Participative Management

A fairly recent development in some academic libraries is participative management of one form or another. This system involves staff at all levels in decision-making processes and circumvents the time-honored "pyramidal" structure of library administration, in which decisions were made at the top (usually by a single individual) and the ramifications trickled down to the ranks. Participative library governance goes by different names, but the two most common are *orbital management* and *quality circles*, pioneered by successful Japanese industries. But Oriental concepts do not always translate well into Western society, and problems can and do tend to arise wherever such systems are in place. Such reorganizations of decision-making and administrative placement in the hierarchy present unique opportunities and a corresponding list of problems. Among the opportunities is the possibility for staff to feel that they have input into decisions that affect their professional lives, which carries a corresponding sense of self-esteem and improved staff morale. Among pitfalls may be the threat posed to administrators, who must share the privilege of deciding on courses of action, and the eventual realistic necessity of pulling rank and saying "We'll do it my way," which negates the concept of "participation" and may cause morale to collapse to lower levels than it was before the innovative, more "democratic" institution of participation in decision-making was announced. Nevertheless, the notion of staff participation in decisions that affect all ranks and levels of the institution is interesting and meritorious enough to bear watching, as experiments in such systems of governance succeed and fail.

"Free versus Fee"

Returning to the library-as-a-business question, one might ask whether information, as a commodity with intrinsic value, should be for sale or whether it should be given freely to those who want it or need it. It has been demonstrated that the United States is a nation divided in two: some might argue that it is two nations, the "haves" and the "have-nots."

If, on the one hand, information is to be given out on request without cost, how shall libraries recover the expense of purchasing, compiling, and packaging that information? On the other hand, even an extremely modest system of cost recovery, by which the library charges fees only large enough to return to it what was spent to acquire the information, will serve the purpose of pricing that information beyond the means of a large segment of the populace. Remember that information is not like logs or hogs: it is something that can be duplicated endlessly without the loss of the original product.

The problem with that prolific information dissemination, some critics charge, is that it cheapens the value of the information. Or perhaps the value remains the same, but the costs and profits change. If nothing is done about this situation, publishers and authors may well decide that they receive too inadequate a return on their initial output and cease providing information at all. The U.S. Copyright Law is under what seems to be almost continuous review in the ongoing attempts to define *fair use*, so that authors, publishers, agents, librarians, students, and the general public feel that their interests and rights are protected. Understandably, a perfect solution that makes all parties happy is never going to be achieved. The debate continues.

Interlibrary Cooperation

Libraries frequently wish to enter into cooperative agreements with other libraries of the same type, or with multiple types of libraries, for mutual benefit. Cooperation is not always entered into out of free will or with enthusiasm; at times, cooperation may be mandated by the state or federal government, or libraries may be lured, seduced, induced, co-opted, or bribed into cooperation, or argued out of their traditional stand-alone attitudes by vague promises of benefits or threats concerning the failure to jump on the cooperation bandwagon.

While it is true that cooperative ventures among libraries potentially create "win-win" situations, whereby all players profit from their participation, experience has shown that some sacrifices or discomfort are necessary on the part of some while a few libraries reap most of the benefits of the sharing, without losing much in the way of access to collections or services. This is not intended to argue against cooperative ventures (many of which offer no choice of action to the participants), but to urge the careful and close scrutiny of what is promised, what is offered, what must be shared or relinquished, and how users are likely to react to changed conditions.

NOTES

[1] *Intellectual Freedom Manual*, 3d ed. (Chicago: American Library Association, 1989), p. 3.

REFERENCE LIST

Asheim, Lester. "Librarians as Professionals." *Library Trends* (Winter 1978): 225-57.

———. "Ortega Revisited." *Library Quarterly* 52 (1982): 215-26.

Birdsall, William F. "The Political Persuasion of Librarianship." *Library Journal* 113 (June 1, 1988): 75-79.

Braunstein, Yale M. "Library Funding and Economics." In *Rethinking the Library in the Information Age, Volume II*, pp. 201-14. Washington, D.C.: U.S. Department of Education, Office for Library Programs, 1987.

Buckland, Michael K. *Library Services in Theory and Context*. 2d ed. Berkeley, Calif.: University of California Press, 1988.

Bush, Vannevar. "As We May Think." *Atlantic Monthly* (July 1945): 101-8.

Gates, Jean Key. *Introduction to Librarianship*. 3d ed. New York: McGraw-Hill, 1988.

Josey, E. J., ed. *Libraries in the Political Process*. Phoenix, Ariz.: Oryx Press, 1980.

Lacy, Dan M., ed. *Freedom and Equality of Access to Information: A Report to the American Library Association*. Chicago: American Library Association, 1986.

Martin, Lowell A. "Library Planning and Library Standards: An Historical Perspective." *The Bookmark* 39 (Summer 1981): 253-60.

Ortega y Gasset, José. "The Mission of the Librarian." *Antioch Review* 21 (1961): 133-54.

Wasserman, Paul. *The New Librarianship: A Challenge for Change.* New York: R. R. Bowker, 1972.

Wilson, A. "The Information Rich and the Information Poor." *ASLIB Proceedings* 39 (January 1987): 1-6.

4 | Types of Libraries and Information Centers: Governmental

DEFINITIONS, GOALS, AND OBJECTIVES

Governmental libraries and information centers include information agencies operated at public expense for the citizens of the United States or other countries, or for residents of a particular state. They serve federal and state governmental officials as well as the public. This chapter discusses their objectives and goals and the services they provide in fulfillment of their respective missions.

U.S. GOVERNMENTAL LIBRARIES

Federal

The Archival Function. A very important function of the United States government's library and information network is to preserve and facilitate use of archival material. The National Archives collects and arranges such material for effective use by the American people, but its overriding concern is the preservation of documents that could never be recovered or duplicated if lost or damaged. This is not to suggest that the public is unwelcome in any of the archival installations of the government, merely that the charter of their inception is to serve as a resource for government through preservation and availability. All other purposes are secondary. Therefore, service functions are subordinate to preservation, resulting in restriction rather than facilitation of use. The National Archives (technically, the National Archives and Records Service) takes charge of records after the original function for which they were intended has been fulfilled, including all archival documents of the domestic and diplomatic functions of the federal government from its inception and from the final years of the colonial period. The National Archives publishes guides to the use of its documents; provides reference service; and will furnish, on demand, copies and facsimiles of the documents within its trust. It is also the place to go to see originals of such important documents as the Constitution and the Declaration of Independence. Presidential libraries, despite their locations in various parts of the nation, are operated and maintained by the National Archives. Recently controversy has arisen over the funding of presidential libraries. (The Richard M. Nixon Library in Whittier, California, is privately funded.)

National Libraries

The Library of Congress (LC) is not, strictly speaking, a national library, because it was created by and for the legislative branch of the federal government. Nevertheless, LC serves most of the functions of a national library. It is divided into six departments, each of which is subdivided into divisions. The Administrative Department has responsibility for personnel, building maintenance and grounds, collection maintenance, preservation, and fiscal administration. The Copyright Office registers all claims for copyright protection and receives copies of books and other materials deposited with copyright applications. The Law Library provides legal reference and circulates legal materials to members of Congress. This library exists and operates apart from the Supreme Court Library and numerous other libraries in the Washington, D.C. area, which are established and maintained for the purpose of informing citizens and agencies about laws that affect their lives and livelihoods. The Congressional Research Service acts as the reference department for Congress, accepting requests for information, research, addresses, background, etc., and responding to members' demands. The Processing Department includes both descriptive and subject cataloging divisions, the Decimal and Library of Congress classification offices, and the card division. It administers the sale of printed cards, MARC tapes, bibliographies, and other reference tools. The Reference Department provides service to government agencies, libraries, and individuals. Outside of these departments, various divisions have been established to provide various specialized services, such as the Division for the Blind and Handicapped and the Rare Book Division.

The Library of Congress was founded in 1800 to serve as the information resource of the two houses of Congress. Funding for LC is primarily from congressional appropriation, consisting of tax dollars from Internal Revenue sources. Administratively, LC is governed by the Librarian of Congress, who is appointed and serves at the pleasure of the president of the United States, with the consent of the Senate.

Of interest to information professionals are the various ongoing projects of the LC, such as *The National Union Catalog (NUC)*, which attempts to serve as a collection and locational device for those seeking hard-to-find volumes. Major research libraries submit tapes of their holdings, which are assembled, organized, and alphabetized by division personnel. If, for example, a scholar or researcher were unsuccessful in locating a particular book, in the Washington D.C. area, by consulting the *NUC*, he could discover that the book is held by a library whose encoded "address" is CtY. The code printed in the front of each *NUC* volume reveals that "CtY" stands for Yale University Library (Ct = Connecticut; Y = Yale). The researcher would then call, write, or FAX that library to see if arrangements could be made to send the book, copy the book, copy a portion of the book, or make the book available in-house for a personal visit.

Another union catalog published by the government is *The Union List of Serials (ULS)*, which is similar to the *NUC* but covers serial titles, defined as works designed to be published in series with no predictable end. This category generally comprises magazines, journals, newspapers, and other "regular" issues. There is debate over whether annual publications (e.g., *The World*

Almanac) qualify as serials, but definitions are generally consensual. Someone seeking to consult a specific title but unable to get hold of it locally could consult the *ULS* and find out where it might be available and what issues are available.

Each time the office of Librarian of Congress falls vacant, discussion and controversy arise over whether the next appointee should be required to possess library education or practical library experience. Throughout the past few decades, the Librarian of Congress has been a prominent scholar. Evidently the assumption has been that the system provides for numerous administrative officers who are competent to run a library system, but the person at the top must or should be a "name," whose prestige and recognition will attract funds, grants, and respect. The American Library Association, together with the National Commission on Libraries and Information Science and other organizations, have been conspicuously unsuccessful in efforts to influence this presidential appointment or to persuade the various administrations of the importance of appointing a professional librarian, a minority group member, or a female to this position.

There is also controversy over the mission of this, the largest library in the world (depending on how and what you count, there are anywhere up to 100 million items in its collections). One faction holds that this tax-supported and publicly operated library ought to be a truly national library. However, while many services of LC are available to individuals who request them, service to Congress is still top priority for the library's staff.

The library has grown at an astonishing rate because, by law, one copy of each publication copyrighted in the United States must be deposited in LC and retained. In addition, there is a tremendous influx of government documents, foreign exchange publications, and serials each year. Almost nothing is removed and there is little or no weeding permitted by law. It will come as no surprise, therefore, that space considerations, merely to house the burgeoning population of publications, are of great importance. Also, LC's acquisitions are not limited to books, serials, and other printed publications in English. The mission calls for the accumulation of federal and state documents, foreign language publications, manuscripts, maps, photographs, various formats of art, sheet music and scores, films, videocassettes, audiocassettes, discs, wire recordings, etc.

The Library of Congress also provides for the information and research needs of other branches of government. Scholars from all over the world visit LC to conduct research, as do librarians, museum curators, students, tourists, foreign visitors, and the general public (despite the fact that this is technically not a public library). One glaring omission is that LC provides no services to the young, except indirectly, through collections of teaching materials for use with children. While there are ample materials available to be used with children, there are few designed for children to use on their own. Pressure from the library community for LC to expand its coverage beyond adult-oriented materials has thus far been without result.

One major thrust of LC has been interlibrary loan. Through this program, books and other materials are lent to participating libraries for specified lengths of time for the use of specific requesters. In recent years electronic access to information has in large part cut into the cumbersome, slow, and expensive process of shipping books around the country (or the world). Today, it would be quite simple to mail or FAX information (or whole books' worth of information) from any point to any other point if it were not for considerations of copyright infringement. It is now possible (and even routine) for a library to send an electronic copy of a book (or even a paper photocopy) to another library and still retain the original for use by its patrons. However, in such a transaction, whereby the book now exists in both libraries, there is no compensation to the publisher or the author. Publishers and authors are at some pains to preserve their economic interest in their books, copying and sending books, and various schemes are being worked out to maintain their rights when books are copied and transmitted so that this practice can continue without harming publishers' interests. A system now in place in Great Britain, Canada, and other countries provides compensation to parties with financial interests in transactions of this type, on a system of payment per use. The sticking point in such a system is *fairness*, which will probably never be agreed upon, by all concerned. The problem remains unresolved at this time and makes it difficult for libraries to lend and borrow freely and for users to get what they want without spending time, money, and effort.

The National Agricultural Library (NAL), located just outside Washington, D.C., collects materials about agriculture and related subject areas. Almost two million volumes comprise the NAL's collection of materials, including serials, books, pamphlets, and technical reports in dozens of languages. The card catalog of former times has given way to online access and the AGRICOLA database. NAL takes part in interlibrary loan, photocopies report literature and journal articles, and provides a bibliographical service to employees of the Department of Agriculture. A broad network connects NAL electronically with hundreds of university and college libraries, state agricultural experiment stations, and microfilming projects. NAL compiles and publishes monthly the *Bibliography of Agriculture*, an index to agricultural literature worldwide. Many of the documents available for sale by the Superintendent of Documents are about agriculture and are provided at low (subsidized) cost to the public.

The National Library of Medicine (NLM), also located in suburban Washington, was once called the Library of the Surgeon General of the United States. Over a million books and pamphlets, supplemented by what may be the world's largest collection of medical journals, are available to the federal government, the states, the medical and allied health communities, and the public at large.

The National Library of Medicine has published *Index Medicus* for over 100 years, providing comprehensive access to medical information from all over the world in a variety of formats: print, computer output microform, and the comprehensive MEDLINE database. Professional literature analysts work full-time to produce such publications, with the goal of providing easy and full access to medical literature. This is extremely important in present times, as so many of the current "hot" issues are medical in nature (e.g., AIDS, famine, the "greenhouse effect," drug abuse, smoking).

Literally hundreds of departmental and bureau libraries, serving the legislative, judicial, and executive branches of government, are located in Washington, D.C., and around the world, operating to fill the special needs of various divisions of the United States government. Examples are the United States Information Agency and the United States Information Service Libraries, which provide information about the nation and its people and government abroad; the United States Supreme Court Library; the Smithsonian Institution Library; and the Department of Education Library, a recent outgrowth of governmental restructuring. Military libraries, consisting of both professional and recreational reading materials, are found wherever the nation's fighting forces are located.

National Commission on Libraries and Information Science (NCLIS)

This organization is not a library, and does not possess one, but its goals involve the promotion of libraries in the United States: (1) to meet the basic library and information services needs of local communities, (2) to provide special services to special constituencies, (3) to serve those previously or currently unserved by local library service, (4) to strengthen existing statewide resources and systems, (5) to provide basic and continuing education of personnel to implement programs, (6) to coordinate existing federal programs of library and information science, (7) to encourage entities in the private sector to become active partners in developing a national program, (8) to establish federal responsibility for coordinating a national network, and (9) to plan and implement a nationwide library and information network.

LIBRARY FUNCTIONS OF THE STATES

In one sense, the states' library systems function somewhat like smaller versions of the federal system. Just as the Library of Congress and all the other federal libraries exist to serve the needs of the legislative body (Congress), the judicial branch of government, the executive branch, and the citizens of this nation, so the state libraries exist to serve their legislatures, judiciaries, executive branches, and citizens.

While there is only need for one federal library network, there are fifty state arrangements, not to mention those in territories and possessions of the United States. Each is different and unique in its services and configuration for delivery and implementation of those services.

Each state has an apparatus of library and information services for the benefit of the state government, which comprises three branches: executive, legislative, and judicial. State libraries are not easily classified by function, because, as a result of tradition, local needs, historical accident, and politics, they have grown into a "patchwork quilt" of types. For example, one may find a considerable diversity of names by which state library agencies are known: the Public Library Service (Alabama), the Department of Libraries (Oklahoma, Vermont), The Department of Libraries and Archives (Kentucky), the Department of State Library Services (Rhode Island), the Department of Library, Archives and Public Records (Arizona), the Division of Libraries (Delaware), the Division for Library Services (Wisconsin), the Division of

Public Library Services (Georgia), the Division of Library Development and Services (Maryland), the Library Commission (Mississippi, Nebraska, West Virginia), the Board of Library Commissioners (Massachusetts), the Office of Public Libraries and Interlibrary Cooperation (Minnesota), and the mundane but descriptive State Library (in most states not previously listed). Sometimes, the State Library and one or another of the above titled agencies combine their functions. In Alabama, for example, the State Library is the agency charged with serving the information needs of state government and the legislature's two houses, while the Public Library Service, as might be inferred from its title, backs up public library collections and provides a range of special and extension services to the population of the state.

These agencies are so different for a number of reasons, including history, geographical location, statutes, and the legal status of the agency. Frequently, the position of the State Library in government will determine a range of matters, from the individual to whom the state librarian reports to the range of services to be provided by that agency by law. In some configurations, there is a State Judicial Library, which serves as the Supreme Court's information and legal resource and has no administrative linkage to the State Library at all.

The following services are provided in some manner in every state, with differences occurring in responsibility and administration: (1) library service to state government, (2) a book collection, (3) a documents depository collection, (4) information and reference service, (5) legislative reference, (6) law library service (although this is frequently provided and administered separately from other services), (7) genealogy, (8) state history (each state library agency maintains a large collection of materials for historical research), and (9) liaison with institutional libraries (e.g., those in prisons, mental health facilities, dependency treatment centers, jails, etc.). Some state libraries provide all of these services, to all three branches of government, under a centralized administration, but across the nation there is a dismayingly diverse "patchwork quilt" of administrative patterns and arrangements, with each state trying in its own way to both provide service to members of state government and respond to the general library needs of residents.

CONTEMPORARY ISSUES FOR
FEDERAL AND STATE LIBRARIES

Many issues trouble federal and state library agencies in the 1990s. Following are a number of these:

- Should the Library of Congress be recast as a national library, and what should its responsibilities be?

- How should presidential libraries be funded?

- How can the information profession best influence the selection of appointed officials in governmental libraries and information centers?

- Where does financial responsibility lie for library service to the nation's citizens? Are such services a matter of local concern, or are there legitimate roles for state and federal governments?

- Should the "National Library" be a truly public library, as it is in Great Britain and elsewhere, or should the "Library of Congress" remain what its name implies?

- Should the State Library Agency take leadership in the state and serve as lobbyist for library/information concerns?

- What is the responsibility of national and state libraries for equalizing library service to citizens throughout the country?

- Should libraries concentrate on keeping up with rapidly changing technology, or are they doing best by their constituents when they buy as many of the materials they are requested to buy as possible?

- Should "English-first" be the rule in American libraries, or is there a legitimate place for foreign language materials and services?

- What is the duty of a state library agency regarding minority concerns in libraries throughout the state?

- Should federal and state library money be used for the erection and improvement of library buildings, or should it be concentrated on improving services and collections?

- Are regional and/or multi-county library systems more efficient and cost-effective than the present haphazard system of local libraries? If so, how should state and federal government work to develop such systems?

- How can the persistent problems related to copyright be resolved in ways that are just and fair to authors, publishers, readers, and libraries and information centers?

- How should new technologies, such as facsimile transmission, be used to send information and printed material among libraries?

- To what extent are automation and other aspects of the new technology of value in solving library problems?

- What is the value of research into the problems of libraries. Is such research a valid concern of federal and state libraries, or should it be left to the academicians?

- What are the proper respective roles of the public and private sectors in ensuring the fullest availability and distribution of information?

- How will or should federal and state budget priorities affect the shaping of federal and state policies on disseminating information?

- Does the Freedom of Information Act extend to electronic media?

- How does the Paperwork Reduction Act affect libraries and other information agencies of federal and state governments?

- Has information technology outpaced governmental policies designed to manage data? If so, what can be done about this?

REFERENCE LIST

Federal Libraries and Information Centers

Bearman, Toni Cargo. "National Information Policy: An Insider's View." *Library Trends* 35 (Summer 1986): 105-18.

"Federal Agency and Federal Library Reports." In *Bowker Annual of Library and Book Trade Information.* New York: R. R. Bowker, 1961- . See especially Buckley, Francis J. "Federal Government Information Policies: A Library Perspective." In *Bowker Annual.* 31st ed., 1986, pp. 80-88.

Federal Legislative Policy. Chicago: American Library Association, 1987.

Freides, Thelma. "The Federal Information Controversy from an Economic Perspective." *College and Research Libraries* 47 (September 1986): 425-37.

Hernon, Peter, and Charles R. McClure. *Federal Information Policies in the 1980's: Conflicts and Issues.* Norwood, N.J.: Ablex, 1987.

Informing the Nation: Federal Information Dissemination in an Electronic Age. Washington, D.C.: United States Congress, Office of Technology Assessment, 1988.

Levin, Marc A. "Access and Dissemination Issues Concerning Federal Government Information." *Special Libraries* 74 (April 1983): 127-37.

State Library Agencies

Association of Specialized and Cooperative Library Agencies, Subcommittee for Library Functions at the State Level. *Standards for Library Functions at the State Level.* 3d ed. Chicago: American Library Association, 1985.

_____. *The State Library Agencies: A Survey Project Report, 1985.* 7th ed. Chicago: American Library Association, 1986.

McClure, Charles R., ed. *State Library Services and Issues: Facing Future Challenges.* Norwood, N.J.: Ablex, 1986. See especially Engle, June Lester. "State Library Agencies and Library Development," pp. 80-99.

Types of Libraries and Information Centers: Academic and Research

ACADEMIC LIBRARY DEVELOPMENT

Academic libraries in the formative years of colleges and universities were merely collections of books, placed in one or two rooms for the benefit of faculty and students who might use them profitably. Such libraries were small and rarely used, except perhaps in religious institutions, where devotional and other religious materials were used in the course of daily life. Many prominent, philanthropic Americans bequeathed their personal book collections to institutions of higher learning, assisting the development of their libraries considerably, although the motives for such philanthropy and the conditions attached varied greatly. Still, academic libraries in the United States, with only a few notable exceptions, were small, until state and federal legislation, beginning in the 1950s, appropriated funds for library use over and above those which tuition produced.

As previously mentioned, religious bodies that have founded and endowed higher learning institutions frequently have provided generously for library materials and services, although they have exhibited a decided tendency to reinforce through their collections their official doctrines, while at the same time excluding ideas not in agreement with those doctrines.

As colleges and universities grew away from traditional curricula and textbook readings, their libraries tended to expand and diversify, incorporating new disciplines, new techniques, and a host of new formats for recorded information.

Among the many missions of a large university is that of providing quality education to its students, a mission which entails provision of library services. Another proclaimed mission of such institutions, that of pushing back the frontiers of the unknown through vital and ongoing programs of sponsored research, similarly entails use of libraries, but in a different way. In any case, the academic library must assist in fulfillment of the institution's mission if it is to be effective, and it cannot be called effective if it is deemed unsuccessful in carrying out that mission.

Chief among the functions of any academic or research library, regardless of type, is to help the institution to carry out its program of instruction through support of the curriculum. The library acquires, receives, organizes, maintains, and makes available books, journals, electronic services, and facilities that aid in furtherance of the mission. The academic library is considered the core of the university or college setting in which it finds itself, in many situations valued as highly as the teaching faculty.

Academic libraries can be grouped together by at least one unifying characteristic: the primary objective of their services and collections is the fulfillment of the curriculum needs of their parent institutions. Whatever its ancillary objectives may be, the academic library is (or should be) dedicated to maximizing the ability of students to get what they can out of the established curricula of study. This characteristic of academic libraries permits us to speak of them as a group, despite the considerable diversity of their milieux, clienteles, and services.

TYPES OF ACADEMIC LIBRARIES

University Research Libraries

Research libraries are found in major universities offering a variety of academic degrees, ranging from the baccalaureate to the doctorate and beyond. The clientele for such a library is quite diverse, encompassing a student body ranging from beginning freshmen (seventeen to eighteen years of age) to grandparents. The faculty the library supports will similarly be diverse, and the specialized subject areas will cover over 100 disciplines. Because of the vast scope and breadth of the curricula within the parent institution, the range of the research library's holdings and services is also understandably large. Such libraries have departmentalized services, although there is considerable variation as to whether services are grouped and gathered together under one roof, whether they are spread out over the campus, or whether they are divided among numerous, far-flung campuses of the university, with some branches under the aegis of the university librarian and others independently funded and controlled. The staff of research libraries is large and generally includes several librarians who serve (full-time or part-time) as subject bibliographers, charged with development of the collection in response to student and faculty demand.

Public Institution Academic Libraries

Academic libraries can also be categorized as belonging to public institutions or private entities. The distinction may originate in funding, but goes far beyond the mere question of where the money comes from because it affects such areas as curriculum, community responsibility, audiences, services, and collections. Public institutions (like those bearing state names), for example, derive a majority of their financial support from governmental revenues and consequently are accountable to those who contribute to their support. Tuition, a major source of income, is normally subsidized by state or local money, and in any case does not provide enough money to make it possible for the college or university to restrict access or services to those who can prove that they directly support the college. Tuition also fluctuates wildly, and some public institutions charge three or four times the cost per credit hour as others, even within the same state. Whatever the source of financing, the public academic institution recognizes and proclaims a sense of responsibility to the community, taking part in a number of significant ways in the life and affairs of the area in which it is located.

State universities, for example, belong to all state residents. While this does not imply that the selection and provision of services and collections must be carried out with all state residents in mind, all state residents are normally entitled to avail themselves of those services.

College Libraries

There are many four-year colleges in the United States; some are independent and others are components of larger systems. The unifying principle of such institutions may be said to be that there are no (or few) graduate programs of studies, which means that there are few, if any, graduate students. Students generally range in age from eighteen to twenty-two and few returning students are older than their early twenties. This may or may not mean that the range of services and collections one might expect to find is smaller than that of libraries serving research institutions. More concentrated services are addressed to the needs of undergraduate students, while less attention and less money are normally allocated to research sources and materials. These are generalizations, and there are still colleges to be found that have graduate courses, but in the main they do not extend beyond the fourth (senior) year of study.

Private Institution Academic Libraries

Private colleges and universities are supported mainly by tuition combined with bequests, grants, and alumni support. These institutions are thus free from the statutory requirement of having to cater to the expressed wishes of the community and may even have "closed" libraries, accessible only to persons possessing valid identification or credentials as members of the institution's "family." The services and collections offered by private institution libraries tend to be narrower in scope than those of public institution counterparts, as a reflection of the smaller, normally more homogeneous, clientele to be served.

Teacher's Training Institution Libraries

Many institutions of higher education are devoted primarily to the education and training of teachers, although those offering only bachelor's programs are rapidly becoming extinct. The emphasis of their libraries is to serve as a source of materials and services that will be required or desired by prospective teachers. The emphasis, therefore, is on the practical, rather than the theoretical, but this is changing as faculties increasingly feel the need to explain "why" as well as "how" things are as they are.

Community College and Junior College Libraries

Two-year institutions offering associates' degrees in various fields may be called community colleges, junior colleges, or even trade schools. Their students are of two types: (1) those who wish to remain close to home for the first two years of study, before transferring elsewhere to pursue career-related studies and (2) those who view a two-year curriculum as a terminal degree, enough college to qualify for a professional (or quasi-professional) career in a field of study not normally open to high school graduates. The libraries of such institutions reflect the skill-oriented and basic nature of the curricula and tend to de-emphasize theoretical aspects of various studies in favor of pragmatic information and knowledge that will assist students in getting meaningful jobs upon completion of the two years of study.

Parochial and Other Special Institutional Libraries

Several religious bodies maintain their own colleges and universities, subsidizing tuition revenues with "church" money. Libraries in such institutions tend to be relatively narrow in scope, catering to the requirements of the specific curriculum rather than attempting to provide something for everyone. Where such institutions are operated to provide training for clergy, the scope of instruction is narrower yet, and the library's holdings reflect that narrower scope. However, clergy often acknowledge that a well-rounded and adequately prepared modern spiritual leader requires a broad and diversified background, and they add to the traditional devotional and liturgical program of study such elements as social problems, psychology, ethnic studies, sociology, and the humanities. Libraries in such institutions reflect the nature of the institutional philosophy and its place along the conservative-liberal continuum. These factors will determine the level and quantity of provision of materials for enrichment and enlightenment above and beyond the traditional requirements of specific theological training.

Special Institution Libraries

Numerous institutions of higher learning are owned and operated by, or strongly oriented to, specific sectors of society. These diverse types of institutions include those for the blind, the deaf, African-Americans, and members of specific religious groups. The curricula of such institutions are openly slanted towards the rationale for the institution, and those curricula foster particular, specialized library services and collections.

FUNCTIONS OF THE ACADEMIC LIBRARY

Academic libraries are established at the same time that their parent institutions are chartered. The legal status of the library within the institution is sometimes set out specifically in the charter of the institution, but may be part of the by-laws of the board of governors.

Academic library functions will vary considerably with the type of academic institution and with the myriad variables that give each institution its unique "personality." Services and collections cost money — lots of money — and academic institutions, having their own financial problems, must cope with the competing demands of library and other services when allocating funds to make such services available in anything near the desired amounts. Following is a brief discussion of the functions generally carried out by academic libraries.

Carrying Out Institutional Objectives

Academic institutions, regardless of type, can only achieve their teaching objectives when a good, up-to-date library is present. Put another way, an academic institution cannot be said to exist without a library. The academic library frequently has been described as the "core" or center of the institution, because without it few programs could be run successfully. The varied academic objectives of the institution are normally so integral and intertwined with those of the library system that the two entities are difficult to view separately. The library assists the institution in carrying out its objectives by providing materials and information that make possible the diligent and rational pursuit of those objectives.

Supporting the Institution's Instructional Program

Every academic institution offers programs of instruction culminating in academic degrees. It is rarely possible for faculty members to sell or distribute syllabi or reading lists and feel that they have fulfilled their obligations. It is the job of the academic library to provide enrichment materials, both related and not directly related to course materials and topics, as well as a broad collection of materials for browsing, accidental discovery, and independent study. In addition to print materials there is a wide range of non-print ones, for teaching and learning in ways other than reading.

ADMINISTRATION

The administration of the academic library is headed by a senior officer, whose title varies considerably. In different institutions, the title of the person in charge may be Director of Libraries, Dean of Libraries, or even Vice President for Information Services. The presiding officer, in turn, may report to the president of the university directly, to a board, to one or more vice-presidents, to the provost, or to a different person entirely, as the hierarchies of academic institutions have differing structures and spans of control. Such lines of authority affect the library's ability to secure and spend funds in differing ways.

NEEDS OF ACADEMIC USERS

Anticipating the needs of academic library users has always been a serious challenge. The academic institution's curricular offerings should provide the basis, but the ultimate needs of users go beyond the courses listed in the catalogs. These needs are as varied as the users themselves. However, there are generalized norms of academic user behavior, because academic users traditionally had been closely grouped in age, with the presumption of minimum educational attainment. In the past two decades, however, many people have gone "back to college" irrespective of their age, under various lifelong learning programs. Academic libraries stress pragmatic needs (i.e., services and collections) that must be either in place or under development before the academic library may legitimately accomplish its mission and goals. Success or failure in the recruitment and retention of quality library staff play a significant part in the ability of the library to achieve its objectives. A low employee retention rate may reflect nothing more than salary levels, but it also may be a sign of something more pernicious. Unfortunately, the administrators of libraries sometimes are the last to recognize that the problems with the system may originate in the head office. Constant or even frequent turnover and the repeated need to find and train new personnel prevent steady progress.

BARRIERS

There are numerous barriers to the fulfillment of the academic library's objectives and goals as they pertain to maximizing the institution's ability to enhance and facilitate the students' learning experience. Some of these are unavoidable consequences of living and working in the real world, while others depend upon changing academic environments. It is impossible to name all the barriers to a library's drive for excellence, but a few of the more salient are described here.

Costs

Costs are a twofold problem, as the library must first worry about its overall budget allocation and then deal with distribution of that money into priorities for spending. There is no common or universal method of determining how much money an institution provides for library services. Some institutions apportion money according to a line-item budget, in which the current year's amount is likely to be based on the previous year's plus (or minus) some percentage adjustment. Other institutions demand program budgets, whereby the library's eventual pot of money is tied to what it plans to do with it. Still others allocate a certain sum per student enrolled in the institution or base the amount on a formula such as the Clapp-Jordan (see page 69).

The library allocation for academic libraries may range from around 3 percent to over 6 percent of the total institutional budget, with the percentage running higher at strong research universities. Where libraries not part of the general system are present, the budgetary allocation may exceed such percentages considerably. There is no standardization or even any pattern in the methods by which budgets are estimated, negotiated, and secured. In every case, however, the library finds itself competing with other demands on the total academic budget and must justify its request for funds in terms of actual needs.

Despite price breaks and improved technology, automation is very expensive, and one of the first and most important choices of academic library planners may well be between more traditional materials and more technology. Can the budget manage to stretch over *both* the desire to have the latest in computer-based services available to its users and the equally strong wish to retain periodical subscriptions despite annual hikes in subscription prices and postage costs? Recently, all libraries have been victimized by runaway escalation in periodical subscription prices, together with the postage hike enacted in early 1991. Each individual library, assessing its situation and its unique set of conditions, must resolve this problem for itself, although the pressures to reach higher and more sophisticated levels of automation are often compelling and imposed by higher authority within the institution. In the area of technology, serious problems arise when vendor agreements and contracts are breached by the vendors, leaving the academic library with inoperative systems that cannot easily be repaired. Compatibility is another frequent problem because there is still little standardization in component specifications and software, often resulting in computers within an institution being unable to communicate with each other.

Uncertainty

Every actual or potential purchaser of equipment has at one time or another wondered if it is just too risky to buy something expensive and non-returnable, because tomorrow, or the day after that, there might be something better, or something that renders present machinery obsolescent, or something incompatible with present hardware, software, or telecommunications. As a result of this very real and understandable fear, libraries may be paralyzed by indecision, incapable of action lest they make a mistake.

Compounding the problem, even if the library management team is sure that a particular move is the correct one, administration of the institution (who are beset with loudly competing demands for augmented funding) may be hesitant to commit funds. This is a real barrier to progress in solving the academic community's information needs, because no one wants, or can afford, to make a blunder.

Institutional Priorities and Political Structure

Some academic institutions are committed to their libraries' planned, steady growth and development, but others regard the library system as a seemingly bottomless pit, constantly clamoring for more and more financial resources. Because institutional planners must view the big picture, their priorities may, under a given administration or in a given year, positively or negatively affect the fortunes of the libraries. About the only thing academic librarians can do to influence those priorities is to demonstrate the value of a good, efficient library system to all members of the academic community. If the library is perceived as an important, essential part of the university or college, that perception will almost invariably have a positive effect upon budgetary allocation. This doesn't necessarily mean more money, but it will tend to preserve the library's allocation when cuts are made. A related problem unique to academic libraries occurs when faculty from specific departments clamor for increased shares of the library budget, citing the indispensability of certain subscriptions and sets to their teaching effectiveness. Competing demands from intractable faculty departments often leave the library staff with a choice of "robbing Peter to pay Paul" and saying no to budgetary requests in excess of specified amounts. The job of balancing selection requirements and desiderata can earn the library staff the resentment of some faculty members.

Competition for Funding

Some academic administrations, viewing the academic library as a "bottomless pit," may try to capture and retain all available funds not disbursed for salaries. It is not too hard to understand this viewpoint when one takes into account the widely diverse types of academic libraries. Human nature being what it is, attitudes toward academic libraries may range widely even within the same institution. Overall, visionary, long-range concepts of the library's function are most effective when they are shared because funders and practitioners will perceive the same priorities. To the extent that they *are* shared, much may be accomplished, with or without additional infusions of money from other sources. To the extent that they are not shared, dissension and mistrust, quibbling over appropriate avenues for future growth, and disaffection will result. An effective library or institutional manager may not be able to impose personal views as to the right decisions or budget allocations, but must be willing to make the attempt, trying to persuade, not to stifle dissent. Dissent can sometimes be overcome through a frank and forthright exchange of views, but sometimes it becomes necessary to reach decisions based on authority.

Problems with Accreditation

Standards for academic libraries are imposed by regional accrediting bodies, and may be of two types: visionary goals worth striving for and minimal thresholds of adequacy. Goals refer to those lofty and conscientiously pursued benchmarks of excellence that library planners strive for, while minimal thresholds are those criteria for libraries that seem reasonable and attainable, given available funds, or the levels that consensually excellent libraries have attained.

Most academic libraries are governed by an overarching set of accrediting bodies, such as regional associations of schools and colleges, national professional bodies, and statewide associations. A problem sometimes arises from the fact that the regional accrediting bodies accredit institutions in their entirety, while professional standards are based upon some mix of normative criteria and wishful thinking for a specific academic area. National standards for libraries do not take into account specific or localized circumstances, while local and state standards acknowledge prevailing norms, economic levels, and expectations. Standards, in the final analysis, are worth exactly the amount of faith that people have in them. Also, standards must have "teeth" in them so that compliance becomes a matter of importance. Non-compliance should carry penalties that institutions will seek to avoid. Without "teeth," standards are merely guidelines or suggestions that an institution is free to observe or ignore. Over-reliance on standards, on the other hand, suggests rigidity, and some latitude should be built into standards (e.g., probationary periods) to allow efforts to comply to succeed. Rigid insistence on compliance can also lead to collapse of cooperative arrangements when the existing standards are regarded as unattainable.

Professional Organizations for Academic Libraries. Several professional associations and organizations are concerned with the development of academic libraries. Principal among these is the Association of College and Research Libraries (ACRL), to which most institutional libraries belong. ACRL, a unit of the American Library Association, publishes *College and Research Libraries*, a scholarly professional journal dedicated to furthering the aims of academic libraries. Other organizations concerned with standards for academic libraries are the Association of Research Libraries (ARL), the National Commission for the Accreditation of Teacher Education (NCATE), and respective regional bodies, such as the North Central and Middle Atlantic Associations. Specific types of libraries within the catch-all category "academic" have their own professional associations, standards, and journals.

COMMON THREADS AND UNIQUE FEATURES

With curriculum orientation in common, what other similarities can be seen in all types of academic libraries? They all provide reference materials; collections (both general and special); some provision of government publications for the use of members of the academic community; a particular set of unique, archival materials; and sufficient equipment to enable patrons to use the available materials.

Academic libraries in general differ from public libraries in several significant ways:

1. Academic libraries' audiences are normally at least seventeen years of age, while public libraries attempt to serve all members of the community.

2. Academic libraries strive primarily to offer curriculum-related materials first, with "enrichment" resources secondary. Public libraries, normally make no attempt to stock schoolbooks and texts, because it is more important that they commit their available funds to other needs of their clientele.

3. Academic libraries are funded by their parent institutions, generally receiving funds based on line-item or program budgets. The source of such funding is institutional revenue. Public libraries are traditionally supported by taxes, most frequently property taxes at the local level. They are therefore often supplied with funds based not so much on what they are doing, or hope to be doing, but on how much money is available.

SOCIETAL FORCES AFFECTING ACADEMIC LIBRARIES

State Governments

For public institutions, the state legislature determines the basic operating budget for the institution, usually on an annual basis. This will affect the amount and distribution of money available for allocation to the numerous units and sub-units of the academic institution, of which the library is only one component. The legislature also has a great impact on tuition levels (which generate more income) for public institutions. But not only the legislature affects the fortunes of libraries. A pro-education governor, an activist department of education, a suitably contrived lottery distribution, the disposition of criminal and traffic fine money, and other factors may yield unpredictable results (both good and bad) for colleges and universities, and thus for their libraries. A new breed of institution is private in nature, but with state ties, leading to state subsidy. Private institutions may be less strongly affected by the attitudes and actions of state government than are their public sector counterparts, but there are many variables at play.

Federal Government

The federal government has had an on-again, off-again relationship with academic institutions, and, through them, with their libraries. Various legislation (The Higher Education Act; The Library Services and Collections Act) has affected the support levels of institutional libraries and consistency has been lacking. Generally, the federal government is willing to contribute a measured amount (frequently a per capita figure) to the states for distribution to universities, based upon federal/state criteria. Sometimes, however, the federal government's expressed needs (or those of a particular presidential administration) do not permit it to continue such funding. At various times in the past quarter-century, administrative officials have attempted with varying success, to impound or rescind scheduled amounts of federal aid to libraries. The government, therefore, has proven to be a somewhat shaky ally of libraries in higher education, in an environment in which competing imperatives and effective lobbyists have diverted or channeled earmarked funds for higher education into other budgetary priorities, such as defense spending, social entitlement programs, or retirement of the alarming and growing national debt.

General Economic Conditions

Various national economic conditions affect academic institutions and their libraries. A significant rise or fall in the national birth rate will eventually affect the available pool of college-aged students. Fluctuations in the Dow Jones average, the relative availability of student loan money and associated interest rates, year-end figures for unemployment or inflation, and the amount required of the federal treasury for social welfare are only a few of the factors that can affect academic libraries' financial health. On the local level, plant closings, a severe winter, high unemployment, or a disproportionate local rate of inflation can have an impact on any academic institution's ability to attract and retain students. The number of students enrolled and the revenues that their tuition generates drive the income of the institution, which, in turn, has a tremendous effect on library income.

Politics and the Electorate

A phrase increasingly heard these days is "taxpayers' revolt." A public institution whose politics, faculty statements, policies, or student activities are displeasing to a majority of the people may lose community support, or find that members of the board of governors are changed at the next election, or that even appointed members' tenure is threatened. While most academic institutions, both public and private, seek to avoid confrontational politics, too often their public image becomes tarnished by bad press or public relations, leading taxpayers to wonder whether they wish to continue to fund higher education at the same level. Of course, the image may also be positive, and colleges and universities may find that community approval has led to augmented revenues. Frequently, however, the academic library finds itself obliged to get along with less, or a static amount of money, while the cost of materials, labor, and supplies continues to rise. Such variations in revenue are unpredictable, and academic librarians normally must cope with the same fiscal upturns and downturns as do their parent institutions.

The University or College Administration

The personality and leadership style of the president of the institution and of various other higher administrative personnel may be a strong determinant of both the funding and the service provisions of the academic library. A strong president may be more successful in securing adequate budgetary provisions from the state legislature or enlisting the support of the governor. Similarly, a strong administrator is generally associated with outside sources of funding, which enhance academic institution budgets considerably. A president and an administration with a visionary concept of where the institution is, and where it ought to be, may contribute to adequate funding levels for such matters as personnel, automation of services, collections, and salaries. Without the leadership and unwavering support of the institution's president and administration, an academic library faces an uphill battle when it seeks the funding to achieve its mission of service to its community.

Trends in Science, Technology, and Scholarship

Like most disciplines, science is cyclical, enjoying a heyday for a while and then receding somewhat, as societal trends emphasize other aspects of community life. In the late 1950s, American science and scholarship received a welcome boost when the nation realized that the Soviet Union had forged ahead in aerospace technology and was threatening to achieve parity in military weaponry. During the ensuing three decades the desire to achieve scientific parity to, or dominance over, its competitors has caused America to place a higher value on innovation, tempered somewhat by a national reluctance to fund military activity and a slow but steady renaissance of interest in the humanities.

The impact of these long, slow trends upon academic libraries has been difficult to assess, but in general they have led to an expressed and powerfully felt interest on the part of academic libraries to acquire more books, secure more periodical subscriptions, have access to more electronic databases, install ambitious integrated computer systems, and attempt to provide a host of other services.

Shifting Priorities

Sometimes budgetary constraints have resulted in static or even declining staffing levels in order to facilitate other improvements in library services. When new academic departments are established, the implications for the library seeking to reflect curricular needs are significant. Similarly, the elimination or merging of departments reflects major shifts in institutional priorities, and the library must keep pace.

Anyone who still thinks that automation of services permits libraries to reduce staff to a skeleton crew of technicians hasn't set foot in a library lately. Still, academic library budgets have risen only modestly, while the expenses of computerized systems and the inflation-driven costs of virtually everything else have escalated dramatically, despite certain demonstrable savings in manpower arising from automated systems. It is frequently in the expensive budget area of personnel that academic libraries decide to cut back.

Another casualty of such forced choices has been the number of hours the library is open for business. Not that long ago, most academic libraries boasted long hours, and more than a few featured twenty-four-hour study facilities for most of the week. Today, many libraries have reduced weekend or evening hours as a tradeoff necessitated by declining funds and shifting priorities.

Publishing Trends

The selection or variety of materials available in academic libraries is not always dictated by available budgets and expressed student and faculty demand. Another very real consideration is that one cannot buy what is not (or what is no longer) available. In this sense, therefore, current library purchasing of materials is a reflection of financial decisions made by publishers and distribution agencies. The cost of books continues to rise; discounts offered by wholesalers vary extensively; and publishers have found that their backlists are smaller, due to adverse consequences of the shifting tax laws of the nation. Libraries often find themselves obliged to try to meet the current year's subscription costs for serials with the previous year's budget, necessitating the cancellation or suspension of many titles, with an overall deleterious effect on scholarship. Frequently, academic faculty are sent lists of journals currently taken in their areas of expertise and asked to mark all titles they can get along without.

Cooperation

Partly as the result of the problems detailed above, academic libraries have entered into numerous cooperative arrangements, seeking to take advantage of any economies of scale that might lead to the enhancement of their purchasing power. Examples of cooperative efforts among academic libraries are various forms of networking for interlibrary loan; "last copy" storage, by which all member libraries may have access to out-of-print books housed in one member's library; and preservation efforts, generally extremely expensive, in which materials which have fallen or are falling victim to rot, mildew, decay, flooding, smoke damage, and the like are preserved and rehabilitated for common use.

Another factor that spurs cooperation is that academic librarians have persuaded their administrative bodies that it is "use" and not necessarily "ownership" of materials that counts with users. Because it is normally unimportant whether the book in one's hands belongs to one's own institution or to another, users have convinced libraries that it is beneficial (despite inevitable drawbacks) to enter into cooperative arrangements with other institutional libraries so that resources may be shared. In addition, the federal government has offered "sweeteners" to spur and encourage interlibrary cooperation, sometimes actually paying for the costs of such services as interlibrary loan, reciprocal photocopying arrangements, reciprocal borrowing, and regular pick-up and delivery route service.

Automation has generally made cooperation both easier and faster, since it is easier to move electrons around than it is to shift books, papers, or disks, and far easier than attempting to transport people from where they are to where the materials are housed. The application of technology to the problem of interlibrary cooperation has not only facilitated that cooperation, it has been the factor making it possible at all for many institutions. The prospect of being able to have something *and* give it away at the same time makes everything easier.

As with all forms of voluntary cooperation, each participant must be satisfied with the arrangement or the compact that was entered into. Academic libraries who enter cooperatives freely, but come, rightly or wrongly, to feel exploited, undercompensated, or misused, will become first disaffected, then alienated or resentful, and will soon seek to dissolve the partnership so hard won after so much negotiation.

Other types of cooperation are union lists and catalogs, centralized or cooperative purchase and acquisition plans, centralized processing and storage, interlibrary loan agreements, reciprocal borrowing, cooperative reference networks, and cooperative computer networks. The growth and development of large systems such as the Online Computer Library Center (OCLC) in Dublin, Ohio, and the Washington Library Network (WLN), in Olympia, Washington—information utilities that facilitate union catalogs and cataloging—have made sharing relatively easy in principle. A persistent problem, however, is participants' attitudes. It remains a moot point whether library staffs want to share and whether sharing agreements will leave them feeling exploited or undercompensated. Each arrangement works to the benefit of all players if expectations are clear and motivations are above board. Disillusionment, however, can lead to abrupt collapse, and to enter into cooperative agreements without a generous amount of prior thought and discussion is risky.

Foundations, Grants, Gifts, and Bequests

Academic libraries are increasingly dependent upon funds from outside the normal sources of budget and tuition. Various foundations, both public and private, offer grants that facilitate libraries' automation projects, bibliographic instruction capabilities, and collection development. Specialized foundations sometimes make available funds for such efforts as minority development (e.g., African-American studies departments and collections) or ethnic studies. This is frequently a function of the institution's milieu and student body. Giving is increasingly supported through fund drives, phonathons, and direct appeals, by which alumni and friends of the institution are importuned to contribute not just to the university's or college's general fund, but to the library system in particular. Earmarking of such funds may even be quite specific, and the donor is often entitled to specify that the gift be devoted wholly, or in part, to establishing or supporting a particular service or collection in the library. Sometimes prominent members of the academic community (e.g., basketball coaches or football heroes) help to secure money for institutional libraries by lending the prestige of their names and their direct appeals to fund drives. Occasionally, such non-recurring windfalls as bowl-game receipts may be channeled from the general fund into the library, if persons of great influence make it their business to lend support.

Another form of funds and donations lies in the willingness of an increasingly growing number of institutions of higher learning to request that alumni and others write (or rewrite) their wills so that, upon the person's death, the university or college receives a library or collection or an annuity, the proceeds of which will endow the academic library. It is not always easy for those in academia to adopt such aggressive and unfamiliar new sources of seeking funding, but the combination of necessity and a growing assertiveness of those who once felt safe in their ivory towers has resulted in the tapping of such fertile sources for growth.

Student Enrollment, Values, and Attitudes

The number of persons enrolling at a given institution fluctuates from year to year, unless an intentional cap is placed on admissions. This is the result of both prevailing economic conditions and student response to university and college recruitment efforts. Some libraries in institutions of higher learning are rewarded, at least in part, as a direct result of enrollment, meaning that the more students attend the institution, the more dollars go into the library's budget. Other libraries receive a fixed or variable percentage of the overall university or college budget each year. This is sometimes a problem, as it implies that the budget of the library system is not tied to what it is doing, or seeks to do, for its community, but rather to the size of that community.

Another concern of the university or college library is how it is perceived by students and faculty. In some institutions, the library is literally the hub of the campus, and most students, faculty, and staff pass through its portals and use its services and collections on an almost daily basis. In other institutions, for a great variety of reasons (e.g., location, hours, poor collection, inadequate staffing, concern for personal safety), the library is used regularly by only a minority of students, faculty, and staff, with the majority finding the materials, services, and study space needed elsewhere. Frequently, when this is the case, the librarians are not doing an adequate job of providing for the scholarship needs. Where this is a matter of policy or staff attitude, it can be remedied fairly quickly by effective administrative action. Where the failing is directly attributable to the lack of money, a solution is more difficult to find. Still, it is empirically demonstrable that there is more support for a library where the will and the effort are in evidence, even though money is inadequate, than there is for one in which the money is available but the public service staff lacks sufficient initiative or the attitude requisite for the library to achieve its goal (and only real justification for a claim on university funds): effective response to informational or bibliographic needs.

Changing values are another variable in the determination of the funding levels for libraries. Today's academic coursework tends to require a considerable amount of outside reading, and frequent free choice of topics, which calls for the library to make available a broad-based and wide-ranging collection of materials. In institutions where graduate study is part of the curriculum, this availability of such materials is a necessity.

Availability of Other Libraries

Each academic institution finds itself in a unique geographic situation. Some exist within urban environments, where other libraries, which may be richer in some subject areas, are accessible electronically, through public or private transportation, or even on foot. Other institutions are located in semi-rural areas, where there are no other libraries of any size and resources, and it takes considerable time and effort to reach larger libraries. The relevance of this last point to academic institution libraries is that those virtually alone in their communities must work harder to provide an adequate range and variety of materials for all within their "families," while those surrounded by other libraries (given reasonably cordial relations and reciprocal borrowing privileges) may relax in some areas of collection building while emphasizing others. Since no library can afford to acquire, everything, automated networks and a cooperative spirit can render distance technically irrelevant, as long as there are both a willingness to share and the funds to make sharing possible.

CONTEMPORARY ISSUES FOR ACADEMIC LIBRARIES

Academic libraries today are confronted by numerous unresolved issues, concerns, and debates. The following is only a representative sample:

- Enrollments may fluctuate at most institutions of higher education, but the general trend is steadily upward, leading to greatly increased demands upon services and collections (not to mention staff). Assuming steady or diminished budgets (after figuring in inflation), where should an academic library trim its budget (e.g., personnel costs, print materials, computer equipment) so that the greatest number of the institution's community is best served?

- It has been estimated that the total amount of recorded knowledge (regardless of format) doubles every twelve years. This means that the total of materials available to libraries in 1991 is approximately twice that in existence as recently as 1979. This progression implies that today's libraries have available to them only about one-half of what there will be by 2003. The economics of this calculation are staggering, for budgets of academic libraries tend to increase very little each year. Selection of library materials, therefore, becomes increasingly important as the array of candidate materials expands. How shall these selection choices be made?

- Automation, a trend that cuts across all types of institutions but is especially prevalent in academic libraries, has caused institutions of higher learning throughout America to commit major portions of available dollars to automating their systems, leaving diminished resources available for traditional services and the staff, and little seed money for other innovations. Some writers have insisted all along that the money spent on expensive new automated systems would be better spent on buying more books, newer books, and augmenting periodical holdings.[1] Are they right?

- The costs of library equipment and materials continue to rise, but salaries and other compensation costs are consuming ever-greater shares of the library budget. Some studies have attempted to demonstrate that libraries that expend the greatest share of their budgets for salaries are those considered "best" by their users. Employee satisfaction is tied up with the expectation of augmented paychecks each year and the presumption is made that satisfied employees provide higher quality services than disgruntled ones. Poor raises, or no raises at all, tend to result in the departure of key employees, failure to attract the best and the brightest, and demoralization among those remaining. For this reason, costs of salaries usually grow faster than those for materials and services. The issue is a question of balance between the demands of users to have the services and collections they want to find in the library and the competing need for good salaries to attract and hold quality staff.

- Most institutions of higher learning are responsive to changes in society and the academic environment, and sensitive to demands for new programs and new courses that did not exist (and/or were not needed) a decade or two previously. Such programs, which may extend from various ethnic studies disciplines to new branches of science, require extensive research collections of materials, both print and non-print. The costs of acquiring and organizing these materials are frequently borne simultaneously with the initiation of the new offerings, and severely affect traditional and pre-existing library services. Where no special funding for such programs and new courses is forthcoming, the library finds that it must slice its "pie' into more pieces to accommodate the new, in-demand programs. This may be handled fairly well, or may have the effect of strangulation upon other programs currently not as much in demand.

- Faculty members in their respective disciplines are not always patient, understanding, reasonable, and forgiving when library staff bibliographers charged with assisting development of collections in their areas inform them that some acquisitions are impossible or must be subject to lengthy delays because of funding problems. This frequently creates the impression that the library is neglecting some disciplines and areas of study in favor of others. Clearly, such is sometimes the case, but the consequences, in terms of perceived and expressed satisfaction among faculty, may be severe, unless the library takes steps to remedy the situation (for example, by keeping departmental allocations secret, redistributing based on enrollment, or alternation, so that each faculty group may have its turn for special attention). How should the academic library handle this sensitive and tricky issue?

• The decline of the textbook, together with the increasing freedom of students to choose and explore their own topics for inquiry, has led to an enormous increase in the requirement for larger, and more diversified, collections. Independent study calls for availability of many thousands of new materials for background information and for accidental discovery of connections and ideas. Is this a justifiable and necessary expenditure for an academic library's budget?

• A number of absolute and relative measures have been chosen over the years to represent standards of adequacy for academic libraries. Administrators often wish that some formula could be developed that a library director could simply plug specific variables into and, by turning the crank, come up with a minimum number of books (or periodical subscriptions, or whatever) for its particular situation. A good example is the Clapp-Jordan formula for evaluating the adequacy of an academic institution's libraries.[2] This formula offers a simple equation based on sheer size, mission, and complexity of the academic institution: a constant of 35,000 "titles," defined as a minimum number for any academic library worthy of the name, is augmented according to such variables as "major" subject fields offered by the institution and number of graduate concentrations, whereby a specific library's parameters and conditions could be added to some basic constant number to determine the number of books and other materials requisite of a minimally competent library. Unfortunately, attempts at applying such formulae and evaluation instruments have met with general failure, for the simple reason that numbers alone cannot represent adequacy. Therefore, the search for quality standards continues.

A simple instrument permitting a library system, with or without the services of an outside consultant or investigator, to assess its degree of compliance with desired traits of that specific library in that specific academic setting is not possible, even if it is desirable. The main trouble with this meritorious quest is that, with so many random variables at play, it is unlikely that any set of standards, despite the built-in degrees of freedom given them, can ever hope to encompass all academic libraries. Academic libraries, after all, may have many things in common, but in some respects they are as unlike as fingerprints.

• Sooner or later, almost every librarian runs out of available space, or conditions become so crowded that there is not room to house staff, collections, and services comfortably. Library buildings are typically built to house all existing materials, with growth provided for a certain number of years. Almost invariably, however, the actual growth rate of libraries soon outstrips projections, leaving buildings woefully overcrowded. The problem of space is one of the most challenging for academic libraries. Computer storage and microform technology, together with telecommunications, go a long way to solving this dilemma, but much remains to be done.

- Many colleges and universities today consider that, because they are located in metropolitan, ethnically diverse areas, their missions oblige them to serve such populations as a priority interest. This is in contrast to universities located in rural settings, small towns, or other areas, which tend to be more homogeneous. The questions for the institutional library charged with carrying out the institution's urban mission is to determine what changes, if any, are necessitated by geographical, demographic, and social milieu.

- It is obvious that sheer size of a library's collection alone will not and cannot qualify that library as a good one. Any library that accepts all donations uncritically while refusing to throw anything away will find that it is not difficult to discover and announce, when the year-end statistics are tabulated, that it has grown rapidly, at least in terms of holdings. Clearly, quality of the collection is much more important than quantity. Yet statistics are considered quite significant. The issue is whether sheer size has any bearing on adequacy of the academic library's collection.

- How is quality measured? Standards exist; numerous devices are in operation for the identification of "essential" books; checklists of "the best" may be found in the literature of librarianship. Criteria for inventory and weeding are readily available, and there are several reputable "opening day collections," which are designed for matching to existing collections. By use of such tools, three categories of materials are created: (1) if the tool recommends a title and the library has it, that's a "hit" or credit; (2) books recommended but not owned constitute a "want list" for filling in gaps in the collection; and (3) books not mentioned, yet owned by the library, are prospective candidates for review and possible discard. Yet all academic librarians know that a large percentage of their books are unused. An important issue is how to select library materials that will be used, while an ancillary issue is what to do with those materials in collections that are never or rarely used.

- An important decision for any academic library is whether subject collections belong with the students and faculty for that subject, or whether it is better to work towards having all library materials together in one centralized location. Academic libraries employing each of these methods may be encountered in any geographic area, and arriving at the best solution for a specific library will be a twofold process of discussing the pros and cons of the two systems with practitioners, and experimenting to see what works best.

- Many libraries, confronted by a bewildering array of choices, find that it is difficult, or even impossible, to buy extensively in all the new formats while keeping up with current demand for books and paper-bound journals published each year. Therefore, within tight budgets, more books might entail fewer journal subscriptions and vice versa.

- A related set of choice-oriented issues deals with selection of books versus software, microform versus electronic storage, videocassettes versus more journal subscriptions, etc. Since no library can have everything desired or needed, how shall materials be selected, and by whom?

- Few departments are as important, or as expensive, within academic libraries as are laboratories. Academic libraries today maintain and operate media labs, language labs, and computer labs for the use of students. Such labs take up considerable floor space within the building and require elaborate and expensive equipment. Without such equipment, the labs are merely classrooms; with it, the labs become budget-busters, consuming scarce resources and creating security problems (both misuse of library materials and vandalism and theft). Staff allocation with respect to laboratories is another headache for budget analysts and library planners.

Staffing

- Is the best academic library staff one that provides subject specialists in various disciplines, or is it preferable to hire and retain generalists, who can handle numerous types of questions and problems? In other terms, can the library best maximize its mission and goals by hiring and training staff who are narrowly but deeply knowledgeable, or is it better to train and recruit generalists who, while they may lack intensive subject specializations, have good levels of skill in many areas?

- Faculty status is a significant issue for all academic librarians. Becoming a faculty member usually subjects a librarian to the rigors of promotion and tenure criteria, and may require that the academic library employee publish scholarly material in order to be considered for merit raises, promotion, or tenure. Failure to achieve tenure normally results in eventual termination from the institution. Increasingly, library staff members, particularly the professional staff, are being designated (and treated) as faculty. While this is a positive force in the augmentation of the librarian's image, there are problems, First, teaching faculty usually possess doctoral degrees. Their guidelines may prevent promotion for librarians whose terminal degree is at the master's level. Achieving tenure puts an additional hardship on librarians who are being paid primarily to carry out their principal assignments. They are not generally given discretionary time (as faculty are) to conduct inquiry into research topics of interest. Finally, many universities and colleges award faculty rank to librarians without necessarily awarding the salary or privileges of that rank. The trend toward academic rank and status is uneven. At many universities librarians elect to pursue a tenure track, with all the duties and obligations appertaining thereto, or may accept positions as "professional" staff, which frees them from publication obligations but entails professional service and carries the risk of termination at the end of each contract period.

This discussion highlights only some of the current, salient, and pressing issues confronting academic libraries. Subsequent chapters of this book deal with other problems, some specific to a type of library and others more common and general.

NOTES

[1] Examples abound. Two particularly telling arguments come from Will Manley and Thomas H. Ballard. Manley's column, "Facing the Public," graces the pages of the *Wilson Library Bulletin*. In his September 1987 column, he wrote, "Enough is enough. It's time to reassert the importance of collections over databases and patrons over networks." Ballard has been writing essays for years stressing the importance of more and better books over automation. His collected, counterrevolutionary opinions may be read in *Knowin' All Them Things That Ain't So* (Champaign, Ill.: University of Illinois Press, Graduate School of Library and Information Science, 1985).

[2] Verner W. Clapp and Robert T. Jordan. "Quantitative Criteria for Adequacy of Academic Library Collections." *College and Research Libraries* (September 1965): 371-80.

REFERENCE LIST

Baker, Norman R. "A Descriptive Model of Library/User/Funder Behavior in a University Environment." *Drexel Library Quarterly* 4 (January 1968): 16-30.

Battin, Patricia. "Research Libraries in the Network Environment: The Case for Cooperation." *Journal of Academic Librarianship* 6 (1980): 68-73.

Crowe, Lawson, and Susan Anthes. "The Academic Librarian and Information Technology: Ethical Issues." *College and Research Libraries* 49 (March 1988): 123-30.

DeGennaro, Richard. "Research Libraries Enter the Information Age." *Library Journal* (November 15, 1979): 2405-10.

"Guidelines for Audiovisual Services in Academic Libraries." *College and Research Libraries News* 48 (October 1987): 533-36.

Holley, Edward, et al. "Defining the Academic Librarian." *College and Research Libraries* 46 (1985): 462-77.

Moran, Barbara B. "The Unintended Revolution in Academic Libraries: 1939 to 1989 and Beyond." *College and Research Libraries* 50 (January 1989): 25-41.

Peterson, Kenneth G. "This Is Academic Librarianship: The Need for Values." *Journal of Academic Librarianship* 9 (July 1983): 132-37.

"Standards for College Libraries, 1986." *College and Research Libraries News* 47 (March 1986): 189-200.

"Standards for University Libraries: Evaluation and Performance." *College and Research Libraries News* 49 (June 1988): 343-50.

Stieg, Lewis F. "The Library and American Education: The Search for Theory in Academic Librarianship." *Library Trends* (Winter 1979): 353-65.

"University Library Standards." *Library Trends* 31 (Summer 1982): 33-47.

Veaner, Allen B. "1985-1995: The Next Decade in Academic Librarianship." *College and Research Libraries* 46, pt. I (May 1985): 209-29 and pt. II (July 1985): 295-308.

6 Types of Libraries and Information Centers: Public

DEFINITIONS, GOALS, AND OBJECTIVES

define

For purposes of this discussion, a public library is defined simply as an institution funded and maintained at public expense, whose mission is that of meeting and serving the informational and recreational needs of the community through the use of graphic records (not merely to be construed as "books").

GOAL: comty defined

Mission:

Serve w/ collcn

There is considerable variation in public library *goals*, which tend to (or should) reflect the desires and needs of the community, but their *missions* are reasonably similar: to serve the needs of the community through the maximization of the graphic record. If there seems plenty of "wiggle room" within this definition, Jesse Shera, who is credited with coming up with it, probably intended it to be so.[1] Theoretically, one may choose to maximize the graphic record by maintaining the widest collection of traditional books possible, while another person may judge that the most effective way to achieve the same goal is to go easy on the print sources while beefing up the library's collection of computer software, video games, programmed instruction, and compact disk-read only memory (CD-ROM) subscriptions. (If this seems to reflect a puzzling lack of consensus on the part of those who call themselves librarians, then you have arrived at both an understanding of our profession and one of the primary reasons why this book has been written.) It is interesting to note that all efforts made on behalf of their communities by public libraries are done with much the same goal in mind: to serve the community's information needs. The paths chosen to achieve this goal, however, differ greatly.

Goal: to Serve needs w/ diff paths as to HOW w/ what

THE PUBLIC LIBRARY: A CLOSER LOOK

The United States boasts over 8,000 public libraries, ranging from huge and complex systems, with dozens of branches serving millions of patrons to tiny, rural one-person public libraries, serving fewer than 100 persons. Modern thinking favors systems, based on a recognition that no library should try to survive alone. Cooperation (see chapter 3), frequently fueled by federal and state money, has emerged as the dominant pattern over the years. Some libraries have joined federations, giving up their unique identities in favor of larger, more economical units, with numerous distribution and service points able to save money for all participants by taking advantage of economies of scale. A few public libraries have maintained a posture of rugged independence, preferring to "go it alone" rather than link with other libraries, which would necessitate consensus or result in imposed control of decisions and choices or in being co-opted by associations that would connect them to big cities' problems.

Public libraries have been around for over 150 years, and throughout their history most of them and those who have guided them have striven, even in the face of grim economic realities and common sense, to be all things to all people in the communities they serve. Clearly such efforts, meritorious as they may be, have met with mixed success. Changes must be made in goals and objectives, lest the library go the way of the dinosaur, whether for lack of funds, lack of interest, or both. Like all social institutions, the public library *in* cannot and does not exist in a vacuum. It exists in a complex and interlocking *Society* series of environments: political, social, economic, and attitudinal. Most public libraries have varying degrees of trouble with censorship, community control, policies, services, collections, etc. If there is a common factor in all public libraries it is that their administrators are searching ceaselessly for augmented funding.

In most states, public libraries are supported by tax monies, although the mix of property taxes, earmarked appropriations from the state, lottery money, intangible taxes, and the like varies greatly. Public libraries everywhere must rely on the good opinion of mayors, county administrators, legislators, and numerous other elected officials; they must depend on the taxpaying public for their very survival or growth. No consensus is apparent as to what a "free public library" is. Some public libraries hold fast to the time-honored principle that the visitor need not have money to gain admission, while others have begun contemplating a vast range of financial remedies to their problems, from sale of merchandise to non-resident admission charges. Once inside the library, one may encounter considerable variation as to what is provided for free and what for a fee.

Some libraries have over time charged fees of one sort or another to supplement tax dollars. These fees are viewed by some librarians with outrage or loathing, while others may be reluctant to impose them, but do out of necessity, and still others feel completely justified in imposing them. Fees normally augment the disposable income of the library and help it balance its budget. However, there are significant problems and philosophical debates over who should pay and how much.

TYPES OF PUBLIC LIBRARIES

There are many types of public libraries, and the categories are not always distinctly differentiated. Major metropolitan libraries, consisting of main or headquarters buildings and numerous regional or neighborhood branches, are found in all populous cities. Sometimes the system is so complex that regional libraries are installed as middle levels between headquarters and the far-flung branches.

Smaller urban libraries may serve their entire communities from a central location, without the need for and expense of branches, or may have one or more satellite locations in outlying parts of the community. Depending upon geography, money, transportation variables, and strategy, the public library may elect to serve as the hub of the community's information resources or may create a network of overlapping locations designed to bring services physically closer to everyone.

City, county, and multi-jurisdictional library systems that are attempting to provide a rough equality of service throughout a geographical area may elect to serve outlying communities and/or sparsely settled areas without building or leasing branches by means of bookmobiles, direct service by mail, reciprocal borrowing, or, in some communities, through actual pick-up and delivery of materials.

Multi-county libraries are larger administrative entities, serving two or more political subdivisions having a large enough population to render certain economies of scale. These library systems may be of two types. The first provides service to two or more counties, featuring joint acquisition, shared cataloging and processing, reciprocal pick-up and delivery, and communications networking. The other normally requires state and/or federal funding, which compensates a larger library in a multi-county area for contractual services rendered to other libraries, with reciprocal borrowing privileges or a one-card, systemwide arrangement.

Rural libraries are sometimes part of a statewide network and sometimes stand alone, without organizational ties to other libraries. Today, however, even the most remote library belongs to some kind of cooperative system at one level or another, even if the only arrangement in evidence is acceptance of other libraries' borrowers' cards. There are also confederations of independent libraries, which agree to certain shared services but preserve local autonomy and participate in no or little joint planning or pooled resources. Each retains its name, director, and funding, but all voluntarily agree to cooperate in purchases or other services.

Multi-type library networks, whose only definitional commonality requires that they encompass two or more library types in a geographical area to enter into a federation or compact, are called by different names in different states (they are called Area Library Services Authorities in Indiana and Regions of Cooperation in Michigan). Across the United States, one may find arrangements in which public and academic libraries have thrown in together, sometimes even sharing a building, and others which schools and occasionally special libraries have also joined, for reasons of economy, a state mandate, or perceived mutual benefit. One state (Hawaii) even has evolved a statewide system of libraries, in which there are branch locations on a chain of far-flung islands with a central library on Oahu.

AUDIENCES

There is a pronounced difference between actual users and potential users of the public library in any community. Perhaps a "user" ought to be defined as someone who borrows at least one book or film or other material every so often, but there would be disagreement over how often, how many, and in what time period. While no library planner can predict with certainty that, sooner or later, all community members will find themselves in need of library services, academic and school libraries have a reasonable expectation of people showing up. A public library, however, cannot foretell use patterns with any hope of precision and can only hope to anticipate trends. Experiential statistics suggest that, in any community, a percentage somewhere between ten and twenty of the resident population may be called library users. But this, of course, entails some definition of its own, and entails certain assumptions.

For example, shall we count "public library users?" How? Are they anyone who lives in the community? Hardly, for the majority of the citizens either never visit the library building or go hurrying by it or through it on their way to other buildings. Is a user anyone with a library card? Again, this is not a very reliable means of establishing "use" because many people duly sign up for, and receive, library cards, yet they never use them. How about counting the people who enter the building? This is not difficult to do, using turnstiles, scanners, or "clicky-counters," but the results are meaningless, because upon scrutiny a very small proportion of the populace will be seen to account for an inordinately large share of the use. An unemployed or homeless person, for example, may enter the library thirty times a day, six (or seven) days a week, accounting for a significant component of the total monthly "use" statistics, this person is not "using" the library's services each time. The distinction between users and non-users may have something to do with the purpose for visiting the building. Some library buildings have multiple entrances, making it possible to enter the building, walk through, and exit, without ever touching (and sometimes without seeing) any library materials. That this should not constitute use will get no argument. Public restrooms, a warm place to wait, and a convenient landmark at which to meet others may also contribute to the statistics of entry without suggesting "use." Most public libraries have discarded the notion of knowing exactly how many people might actually "use" the library and have accepted the principle that everyone eligible for service is a user, with actual and potential users lumped together simply because they cannot be separated in any meaningful way. Most librarians lament the fact that there are so many potential, but not actual, users out there; they are continually devising schemes to "bring these people in."

For the public library, therefore, it is more practical to think and write in terms of the primary audience and the secondary or potential audience, possibly with a "realistic" audience somewhere in size between the two. The primary audience consists of those who actually make use of those services and materials that distinguish the library from other public buildings, such as the bus station. The secondary audience includes and consists of everybody, or at least *potentially* everybody, while the primary audience is only those who consult, borrow, view, hear, or otherwise deal with library materials. Realistically, the entire taxpaying population of the community supporting the public library through its tax dollars is the potential audience for the library, but the *primary* audience's members are those who actually make use of its provisions. In this respect, public libraries differ from all other types. School and academic libraries have primary audiences of students, faculty, and support personnel, with secondary audiences of varying sizes and natures. Special libraries tend to restrict their intended audiences severely. But public libraries are designed to encompass the needs of everybody. A substantial secondary or potential audience is entitled to use the public library and thus is (or ought to be) involved in selection of services and planning.

A large metropolitan public library, for example, may consider its primary audience to be the residents and taxpayers of the city proper, but because of administrative decisions made years ago during a time of economic scarcity, the secondary audience was defined as composing millions regionally, or even the entire population of the state due to the trend toward regional and cooperative library development. Whatever the characteristics, size, and diversity of the library's audience, however, these factors have broad implications for services and collections.

FUNDING AND BUDGETING

Public libraries receive their funding in a variety of ways across the United States.

Property Taxes

Public libraries traditionally are funded by an earmarked share of local property taxes. This amount is normally determined by enabling legislation at the state level, which empowers local governments to set aside a specified percentage of tax revenues for the purpose of library provision. A major problem of this common form of library financing is that it ties income for the library to community wealth and ability to pay, rather than to the needs of a given library in a given year if it is to fulfill its mission.

Special Local Assessments

Libraries may be funded by or have their funding augmented by bond issues, millages, and other special assessments, whereby the citizens consent to contribute to the establishment and maintenance of a public library through a one-time, episodic, or annual sum set aside from general taxes. Frequently, bond issues are used to supplement property tax revenues already in place.

Intangibles Taxes

In some states and/or communities, a small portion of the income of owners of taxable stocks and bonds (and other intangible properties) is allocated to library provision.

State Appropriations

In 1960, only a handful of state governments contributed to the support of public libraries at the local level. This had more to do with tradition than with thrift, primarily expressed as a pervasive feeling among state legislators that public libraries were strictly local in nature, requiring strictly local funding efforts. Through the years, a combination of federal aid to libraries, the democratic wish to equalize access and provision within states, and changes in attitude towards the importance of information provision to citizens made library funding a common line item in state annual budgets. In 1990, forty-five of the fifty states (90 percent) contributed *something* to the amount received by public libraries within their borders, although dollar amounts of such funding ranged widely from pennies per capita annually to over $45 million a year in New York.[2] Per capita figures are, perhaps, most revealing. While five states still contribute no money whatsoever to local funding, a few states kick in over $5.00 per resident each year. The general trend seems to be upward, although it is affected in unpredictable ways by the attitudes of those in office, prevailing economic conditions, and federal leadership. Resistance to increased property taxes has placed state and federal governments in partnership with local communities, supplying the funds for library provision and trying to achieve uniform access to information for all citizens.

Federal Appropriations

Until the mid-twentieth century, the U.S. government stayed out of local library funding, as it did public education. But in 1956, with the passage of the Library Services Act, which was primarily designed to assist rural communites in building libraries, small amounts of money were made available to localities meeting certain federal guidelines, for the purposes of augmenting services and collections. Federal money was received by state library agencies according to a simple per capita formula, and the state doled out funds according to both federally imposed and state criteria. In 1964, after strenuous lobbying by the American Library Association and other interested parties and because of the pervasive effect of shifting taxation bases from urban to suburban communities, the previous act was broadened by the Library Services and Construction Act to permit funds to be used for the construction of public library buildings as well as for materials and services. Since that time, the federal government has been a somewhat unwilling partner in the three-tiered (federal-state-local) approach to library funding. Recent presidential administrations have attempted to impound or even discontinue funds for libraries from the federal budget. The future of the partnership remains uncertain, as a growing national debt and grandiose defense proposals, together with escalating social entitlement programs, make money for "luxuries" such as libraries a lower priority than heretofore. This issue is unresolved at the present writing and is likely to remain so.

Lotteries, Parimutuel Betting, Penal Fines, Traffic Fines

In some states, library revenues are realized or supplemented by legislative action earmarking a designated percentage of such forms of revenue as state lotteries, parimutuel betting (e.g., racetrack receipts), fines (e.g., traffic citations, criminal fines and judgments), and, until recently, even legalized prostitution (in Nevada). These funds are not normally the sole support of public libraries, but rather serve to augment the amounts appropriated locally or contributed by the state legislatures.

Private Funding

Private funding is uneven but at least present in most communities. For example, some libraries are (or have been) endowed by the Carnegie Endowment or other charitable trusts, while others remain endowed by families, private funds, and corporations. One problem with such endowments is that, where this source is present, there is little or no tax support from the community. Some public libraries, following the lead of their academic counterparts, have begun to solicit bequests, legacies, tax-avoidance gifts, and the like. While many librarians still feel it is bad form to authorize aggressive pursuit of private contributions, others see this as a neglected and potentially lucrative source of additional funds.

SERVICES, COLLECTIONS, AND PERSONNEL

It is normally quite difficult to get a handle on the "will of the people" concerning the appropriate services for which their tax dollars should be spent, especially in heterogeneous urban areas. For smaller communities, the staff and policy makers arguably can be expected to have a better idea of what people would like to read or have available. The smaller the community of users (or potential users), the easier it ought to be to figure out what to buy to please or satisfy most of them. Money is always a limitation and a constraint; frequently, lack of time is also a retardant force on a library's ability to provide services. Librarians seeking to be responsive to their communities of users will attempt to survey those users or consider their feedback in some systematic way, to reveal whether the proper mix of services, collections, and personnel are being provided for the users' tax dollars, and will adjust that mixture if it is incorrect.

It is sometimes lamented that libraries seem to be "preaching to the converted" in the sense that they spend their funds exclusively on those who use their services, while seeming to neglect the great preponderance of citizens who might benefit from libraries but either don't know or don't care what services are available. This approach is sometimes termed "elitist" in the sense that only the few are catered to, while the needs of the many go unmet.

EXTENSION

Extension in public libraries is based on the simple idea that, if people seem unable or unmotivated to come to the main library building downtown, the library, if it wants to attract and secure their "business," must make itself available closer to where they live, work, or shop. Several plans have been implemented over the years to make library extension possible.

Branches

The idea of branches came about in the early decades of the present century. When implemented, it provided for a public library facility within walking (or easy transportation) distance of the populace who could not get downtown or did not wish to. In practice, branches were more generously and liberally provided to neighborhoods in which literacy and reading was high and where the crime rate was comparatively lower, resulting in few branches in poorer neighborhoods. Still, branch libraries became common in big city library systems, sometimes divided according to a pyramidal structure in which the main library had regional satellite libraries, each of which in turn had several branches and storefront outlets under its control. Branches are still a part of most city systems, although the past twenty years have witnessed completely changing neighborhoods and the closing of numerous neighbor-hood branches, often leading to a reduction in the number of branches in existence. Since each community is different, the desire or need for branches is a variable and there is no universal or satisfying formula for determining when (or where) a branch will be needed, utilized, appreciated, or maintained.

Bookmobiles

Bookmobiles and booktrailers are another answer to the question of how to serve the community when its members frequently do not choose, or are not able, to come downtown or to a branch. During the 1950s, 1960s, and early 1970s, many public libraries bought bookmobiles. The advantages of the bookmobile are many:

1. The library system may bring books (and other materials) to the people where they live, congregate, or shop.

2. There is no need to build or buy a structure, or to pay rent or taxes on it once it is in place.

3. By its nature, the bookmobile is a portable branch and is quite easily moved around the geographical area to new or different sites as desired.

4. The library system can test patterns of use by stationing a bookmobile in a certain place and then later determining whether a branch building is warranted at that site.

5. A single bookmobile, on a predetermined route and schedule, can serve several neighborhoods in a single day.

There are also disadvantages:

1. There is always a potential threat of vandalism, but this may be reduced when the bookmobile operates during the day and retires to a secure, fenced or locked area at night.

2. Bookmobiles represent sizeable investments, taking money away from other, possibly more important, segments of the library's budget.

3. A driver and a librarian (in a pinch these may be one and the same person) are detailed to the bookmobile, removing them from the library building.

4. Even the largest bookmobiles have comparatively few books, limited space, virtually no workspace or reading chairs, and can accommodate few persons at any time.

5. Staff frequently complain of being hot, cold, claustrophobic, vulnerable to crime, and cut off from convenient restroom facilities.

6. It takes fuel to move bookmobiles around from place to place. As an example, in the 1974 OPEC oil embargo, which drove the cost of motor fuels up 300 to 400 percent, these notoriously inefficient vehicles became ruinously expensive to run, greatly reducing the number of operational bookmobiles in the United States.

Portastructures

Some communities have invested in small, prefabricated, efficient, and self-contained portable branches which, while they require a plot of land on which to sit, are relatively easy to "fold" or relocate should the need or desire arise. These small, inexpensive, and cheerful structures can be erected and equipped in a single day on any small, flat parcel of available land. While they may not be the definitive answer to the question of how to serve outlying areas of the metropolitan community, they are taking hold as an adequate surrogate for bulky, gas-eating bookmobiles.

Books by Mail

At one time, some state libraries adopted an unusual approach to serving people who do not live near libraries; while this innovative service was discontinued because it was costly, it was an interesting experiment in serving the unserved in largely rural states. Through the use of a tabloid newspaper supplement, which appeared weekly in all city newspapers throughout the state, citizens could enter the numbers of their requests and mail the form clipped from the newspaper to the state library, where requests were filled and mailed out within a few days. The catalog resembled the familiar publications of Marbro books or Publisher's Clearing House, but instead of prices, catalog numbers were shown. Postage for sending the books out was paid by the state library, while the borrower paid the (book rate) return postage. In northern states, or in largely rural areas, this idea was extremely pragmatic, but it ultimately failed because of lack of funding, delays, unavailable materials, and a necessarily limited selection. Still, the idea may return should motor fuel become scarce and/or prohibitively expensive. Today, the primary service of public libraries for home delivery needs is materials to the blind and partially sighted, administered by the Library of Congress and by state library agencies.

Electronic Extension

Changing times have already led, and will increasingly lead, to vast changes in the way in which libraries conduct their affairs. The future promises even more in the way of information transfer. One strong argument in favor of mail service is that it is easier to push books around than to attempt to push people around. It follows that it is easier still, and much quicker, to push electrons around than it is to send books and other materials.

The technology already exists for one to enjoy most of what the library has to offer (a notable exception is browsing contentedly through the stacks) in the privacy of one's home. This assumes that one has or can have access to a television set, a mailing address on a computer system, a telephone, and a modem (a device that converts computer signals to telephone signals for transmission, then reverses the process at the other end). With the new technology, there may soon be little or no need to visit the library when one can, quite literally, send for it!

CONTEMPORARY ISSUES FOR PUBLIC LIBRARIES

• What Business Are We In?

There seems to be a good deal of irresolution among the American library community over a matter of fundamental importance to the way in which our libraries conduct their business. This issue may be expressed simply by the question, "What business are we in?" Are we, for example, in the book-provision business? If so, we should devote our efforts (and the major share of available funds) to

Books info [handwritten margin note]

selecting, acquiring, and providing as many copies of books (and other print formats) as possible. Or perhaps we're in the business of information provision, or some third business, or a mixture of them all. Should we then be committing more of our money and time to answering questions, while de-emphasizing the provision of books. How shall such decisions be reached, and by whom?

If we're in business (literally), then we need feel no shame about charging reasonable rates to recover our costs. Or is our prime function to serve as provider of programs and services for the varied population subgroups within our community? If so we have to go easy on both books and information so that we may do a better job of providing such services.

The profession takes no pronounced point of view on the matter; in point of fact, the literature shows that opinion is as divided as it is passionate. It seems appropriate only to point out that few, if any, other fields or professions experience as much controversy over just what it is they have to offer for public consumption. It follows that the more certain one is of what one's ultimate mission is, the better one can actively pursue that mission, devising goals, services, strategies, and tactics in pursuit of that mission. The typical modern public library, because of the obvious fuzziness of its goals, cannot work coherently toward goal fulfillment because those who shape its ends and propel it into the future cannot agree (or have not agreed to date) on what it is supposed to be or do.

- Information and Referral (I & R) and Advocacy

Referrals [handwritten margin note]

This idea originated in numerous American libraries during the 1960s. The concept was simple: the library is not just a place to get books or information, it is a place to get assistance, referrals, an intermediary, solution of a problem, or whatever is wanted.

Libraries offering this service today (One large public library boasts that its institution is "not just a place to get information; it's a place to get help") ponder the implications and ramifications of the term *help* and have come up with different working definitions, policies, rules, and provisions.

As examples of help, a public library might offer its assistance to the public in (1) selection of a nursing home for an aged parent, (2) sources of free legal advice (but not the advice itself), (3) locations of day care centers in the community, (4) veterans' benefits entitlements, (5) sources of free food for persons who have lost or used up all their food stamps for the month.

One persistent problem with I & R is "advocacy" on the client's behalf, much as an attorney or social worker might fight "city hall" or a private interest on behalf of a client. Sometimes, help means taking a position, working on behalf of the client, and, inevitably, coming into a confrontational situation with those who resist the actions called for. Librarians are not qualified or permitted to provide free legal advice, but they can provide the persistence and the contacts to, for example, make life very uncomfortable for a landlord who is delinquent in providing heat, light, or sanitation. At such times librarians must ask themselves whether such actions constitute violation of the studied neutrality that public libraries have cultivated since their origins. Can a library adhere to the principles and practices of our most cherished documents (e.g., the Freedom to Read Statement, the Library Bill of Rights) and still wear the mantle of advocate on behalf of a needy client? Opinion is divided on this point and the profession continues to discuss it. In the meantime, public libraries providing I & R services are being asked (and asking themselves) tough questions about roles and behaviors.

- Publisher Relations and Royalties

Increasing numbers of publishers protest that the public library, acting under its admitted recreational function as a place to borrow books, should pay royalties over and above the price of the books it buys for its use of them. That is, since the public library may be seen as a collective, where one purchased copy may be circulated to and read by a virtually limitless number of readers (the same is equally true for audios, videos, and compact discs), it would be fair for those libraries either to pay more for their purchases in anticipation of the uses to which items will be put or to compute and forward sums per use of each item circulated (e.g., a small amount for each transaction). Such plans have already been instituted in the United Kingdom and Canada and some interested parties claim that it is only a matter of time before they are enacted in the United States.

- Selection Issues

Which materials should a library buy? Academic and school libraries may justify purchase of classics and "important" titles by invoking the prescription principle (see chapter 3). This principle says that it is the role of the library to buy the "best" materials with the funds available and to avoid, as much as can be determined, the provision of ephemera, lightweight fiction, and "trash." But public libraries, supported as they are by the community at large, ought to take a community's interests, preferences, and tastes into account. Therefore, while the demand principle may fail the test of validity for other types of libraries, it cannot be discounted as the driving force for the public library.

- Minorities and the Culturally Disadvantaged: Outreach

Minority segments of the population in any community, when added together, frequently constitute a majority of the populace. Still, there is ample proof that libraries have not gone all out to identify or serve the perceived needs of minority populations in the community. There are many reasons for this and they vary widely from community to community.

What is a minority? Generally speaking, it is a group within the population at large which may be identified by the possession of

Minority

Only if used

certain common traits not shared by the majority of people. *Minority*, from the library's standpoint, carries two connotations: A specific ethnic group, for example, may be both a statistical minority in a community and particularly in the minority in terms of actual library use. What can and should be done to encourage minorities to use libraries, and under what circumstances will they succumb and respond to the lure of those libraries? Frequently a language barrier prevents full and effective use of English-language library materials; sometimes it prevents any use at all. Another reason that such people are not high-level users of public libraries is that literacy, in any language, tends to be low among immigrants. A very real concern in many areas is fear of exposure (and subsequent deportation) on the part of illegal aliens, who, by being required to reveal their names, addresses, and other information about themselves, risk too much to make it worthwhile to seek to obtain library borrowing privileges. In some communities, there is a widespread perception that the public library is strictly a caucasian or "Anglo" institution, not intended for the use of non-English-speaking persons. Sometimes, the feeling that they are unwelcome when attempting first tentative forays into the library is the result not of attitude or paranoia but of deliberate and xenophobic actions on the part of library staff members. In some neighborhoods, persons of certain ethnicities may be at physical risk should they attempt to cross over into the "turf" of another, ethnically different group in order to visit the public library. Shortages of qualified personnel stem from the inability of graduate library schools to attract many students from various ethnic cultures and train them to do professional library work in inner-city public libraries, even in communities where they are needed most. Such libraries frequently lack staff members who speak the language fluently, or come from the same background and can relate comfortably to patrons on their own terms. [Several years of high school or college Spanish courses, after all, do not automatically equip an Anglo to deal with Hispanics and their needs comfortably.] Finally, there are strong cultural traditions in which parents, who knew nothing of libraries back home, pass along attitudes to their children growing up in American communities. How does the concerned public librarian, eager to demonstrate the philosophical stance that everybody's life is enriched through having a good library close at hand, reach and hold members of an ethnic group?

- Special Groups; Special Needs

As is discussed in chapter 8, many libraries work with special (as opposed to general) audiences, materials, and/or formats. Larger public libraries frequently become "departmental," establishing special departments that act and operate much as do special libraries, except for the administrative control and the eligibility for entry and use. Special departments are frequently established to deal with special patrons, (e.g., the blind and partially sighted, exceptional children, foreign language groups).

All communities change, some more quickly than others. The public ⌒ library seeking appropriate responses to the problems of societal and urban change must continually explore new ideas and new sources of funding and support. When a public library finds that changes have been made in the community's population, economic base, demographics, or attitudes and perceptions, a measured, effective response is called for, with a minimum of delay. The nature of this response, of course, will be a function of the nature of the change and of such variables as leadership, community demands, prevailing staff attitudes, money, and time.

NOTES

[1] Jesse Hauk Shera. *The Foundations of Education for Librarianship* (New York: Wiley-Becker and Hayes, 1972). On page 48, Shera asserts that "the library is an instrumentality created to maximize the utility of graphic records."

[2] *The Book of the States* v. 1 (Lexington, Ky.: Council of State Governments, 1935- .). Biennial.

REFERENCE LIST

Ballard, Tom. "Public Library Networking: Neat, Plausible and Wrong." *Library Journal* 107 (April 1, 1982): 679-83.

Boorstin, Daniel J. "The Indivisible Community." In *Libraries and the Life of the Mind in America*, pp. 115-30. Chicago: American Library Association, 1977.

Braverman, Miriam. "From Adam Smith to Ronald Reagan: Public Libraries as a Public Good." *Library Journal* 107 (February 15, 1982): 397-401.

Dain, Phyllis. "Ambivalence and Paradox: The Social Bonds of the Public Library." *Library Journal* 100 (February 1, 1975): 261-66.

Dowlin, Kenneth. "Technology in the Public Library: The Impact on Our Community." *IFLA Journal* 13 (1987): 39-44.

Hafner, Arthur W. "Public Libraries and Society in the Information Age." *The Reference Librarian* 18 (Summer 1987): 107-18.

Hutton, Bruce, and Suzanne Walters. "Focus Groups: Linkages to the Community." *Public Libraries* 27 (Fall 1988): 149-52.

Johnson, Debra W., and Marsha D. Rossiter. "Planning Library Services for Special Needs Populations." *Public Libraries* 25 (Fall 1986): 94-98.

Krull, Jeffrey R. "Private Dollar$ for Public Libraries." *Library Journal* 116 (January 1991): 65-68.

Martin, Lowell. "The Public Library: Middle-age Crisis or Old Age Crisis." *Library Journal* 108 (January 1, 1983): 17-22.

McClure, Charles R., et al. *Planning & Role Setting for Public Libraries: A Manual of Operations and Procedures.* Chicago: American Library Association, 1987.

Moore, Bessie, and C. C. Young. "Library/Information Services and the Nation's Elderly." *Journal of the American Society for Information Science* 36 (November 1985): 364-68.

Palmour, Vernon E., et al. *A Planning Process for Public Libraries.* Chicago: American Library Association, 1980.

Penland, Patrick R. "Client-centered Librarians." *Public Libraries* 21 (Summer 1982): 94-98.

"Public Libraries." In *ALA World Encyclopedia of Library and Information Services*, pp. 55-75. Chicago: American Library Association, 1986.

Public Library Association. *The Public Library Mission Statement and Its Imperatives for Services.* Chicago: American Library Association, 1979.

Public Library Association. *Standards and Guidelines for Public Library Service.* Chicago: American Library Association, 1967.

Rohlf, Robert H. "Standards for Public Libraries." *Library Trends* 31 (Summer 1982): 65-76.

Van House, Nancy A. "Public Library Effectiveness: Theory, Measures, and Determinants." *Library and Information Science Research* 8 (July 1986): 261-83.

Veatch, L. "Output Measures for Public Libraries: A Manual of Standardized Procedures." *Public Libraries* 21 (Spring 1982): 11-13.

Zweizig, Douglas. *Output Measures for Public Libraries: A Manual for Standardized Procedures.* Chicago: American Library Association, 1982.

7

Types of Libraries and Information Centers: School Libraries and Information/Media Centers

Carole J. McCollough

DEFINITIONS, GOALS, AND OBJECTIVES

The integrated concept of school library media centers (SLMC) that we know today can be defined within the context of educational reform and the standards documents that shaped and nurtured its evolution. The beginnings of the school library movement were in place long before the expansion and growth of public libraries and the American Library Association's birth in 1876. School libraries were established first in New York State in the middle 1800s through legislative action.

These early efforts failed for a number of reasons. First, the collections, which were at best haphazardly assembled, gradually became dispersed into classrooms. Second, the designated teacher librarians had received little specialized preparation or training. Finally, the development of the public library consumed the professional interest of library leadership until World War I.[1]

The increase in school population following World War I and the progress in educational reform movements promoted by educators such as John Dewey gave support to the concept of centralized school libraries administered by specialists trained to work in the schools. The National Education Association provided a catalyst to school library growth through its publication in 1920 and 1925 of Charles C. Certain's reports on school library organization. The reports, which became known as the "Certain Standards," provided detailed recommendations for the establishment, expansion, or evaluation of a school library facility.[2]

In 1924, the North Central Association, the first accrediting agency for schools, developed a matrix for schools to evaluate their library facilities. The "Score Card for School Libraries" made an effort to identify and measure the *qualitative* aspects of school libraries, unlike the detailed, quantitative standards that characterized existing measures.[3] Although the American Library Association (ALA) published several textbooks providing guidance in the training of school librarians, their first national standards document, "School Libraries for Today and Tomorrow," was published in 1943 and revised in 1945.

In 1958, the federal government initiated a series of legislative responses to educational inequities that would have a significant impact on the progress of school library programs and services for more than a decade. The National Defense Education Acts of 1958 and 1964 (NDEA) and the Elementary and Secondary Education Acts of 1965 and 1966 (ESEA Titles I and II) provided grant programs and financial assistance for library resources and instructional materials.

The 1960s ushered in a period of intensive activity in school library growth and development. The federal government initiated the Elementary and Secondary Education Act through Title II (ESEA-II), which provided federal funds "for the specific purpose of establishing and strengthening school libraries."[4]

The state and federal governments have provided significant supplementary funding for school libraries over the last three decades. The library and educational communities have recognized since the early developmental years the impact that deficiencies in staffing, collections, and facilities for school libraries have had on qualitative educational goals. Coalitions and cooperative arrangements among the American Association of School Librarians (AASL), the National Education Association's (NEA) Department of Audiovisual Instruction (DAVI), and the Association for Educational Communications (AECT) contributed to school library development by producing qualitative guidelines: *Standards for School Library Programs* (1960); *Standards for School Library Media Programs* (1969); and *Media Programs; District and School* (1975).

Progress between 1960 and 1975 was further supported by several major research projects funded by the Knapp Foundation and The Council on Library Resources (CLR). The Knapp Foundation Project was developed to study manpower issues in task analysis, professional education, and recruitment. In addition, the Knapp Project provided library media demonstration programs in several states. The CLR Grant funded the School Library Development Project, which provided guidance to states implementing the 1960 *Standards*.

The educational requirements standard for school librarians in the 1960 *Standards for School Library Programs* was based upon the position agreed upon in 1958. The title for school library personnel was not changed until the publication of the 1975 standards document, *Media Programs: District and School*. It was at this time that the term *school library media specialist* came into use.

School media program growth peaked around 1976. The tightening of federal funding opportunities was accompanied by pervasive criticism of public education, a national focus on accountability issues, and the disenchantment of local school districts with the impossibility of meeting the stringent quantitative standards for library media programs set by professional organizations. The change of federal funding from categorical aid to the Education Consolidation and Improvement Act (ECIA) of 1981 (referred to also as ESEA Title IV) was devastating to school libraries. Library media programs found themselves competing with other teaching needs for funding priority. Without the support provided by Title II monies, school districts enacted heavy cuts in library media programs, collections, and staffing.

The publication of the 1988 guidelines, *Information Power*, incorporated a new approach to media program planning, development, and analysis. Media specialist roles and responsibilities are now consolidated to focus on three major areas: information specialist, teacher, and instructional consultant. These descriptors emphasize the librarian's expertise as an informational professional; knowledge of techniques for teaching information retrieval, utilization, and process skills; and ability to perform as a partner in designing curriculum and identifying instructional methodologies that make effective use of a broad range of information resources.

Goals for the library media program identify a site-specific process that is unique to the mission, resources, and institutional parameters of a given district and building. In the area of staffing, *Information Power* recognizes the media professional as key to an effective program. The guidelines call for a certified teacher and library media specialist with competencies in the areas of library and information science education, communications theory, and technology.

Goals for resources and equipment speak to a need to redefine the concept of *collection* in terms of "information services." Library media collections described in *Information Power* must be developed, analyzed, and evaluated in terms of emerging packaging and delivery systems. Collection parameters are limitless, given the potential of information networking liaisons.

The negotiation of networking and cooperative arrangements to provide information access and delivery is fundamental to the paradigm shift illustrated in the new guidelines. It is imperative that media specialists recognize that to collect in one place all the information resources their users request or may conceivably need constitutes an impossible task in the information environment of today. The reality has been described as an essential need to seek information resources beyond the walls of the media center, establish liaisons, and develop new and revitalize old networking agreements and relationships.

Information Power is a qualitative guide to planning. It differs from similar, previous documents in purpose, methodology, and objectives in that it does not purport to set a "standard." The only quantitative measures found in the document must be extrapolated from the appendixes.

TYPES OF SCHOOL LIBRARIES AND MEDIA CENTERS

The library media center in the school ranges from the traditional print-oriented library facility in small or poorly funded school districts and rural areas to the completely automated, fully staffed library media center (LMC). The traditional library facility located in the elementary school may not be staffed by a media professional. If it has a certified media specialist, that person typically provides services in three or more buildings.

These traditional facilities have limited hours of operation and are often staffed by paraprofessional clerks or parents. The collections include few if any materials beyond books. Many of the reference materials, as well as large portions of the recreational reading, may be permanently housed in decentralized classroom collections.

The integrated media type facilities operate under a variety of titles, including library media center, instructional materials center, learning resource center, and instructional media or services center. The variety of descriptors is a direct result of the 1975 standards document, *Media Programs: District and School*, which consolidated the trend towards multimedia materials collections. The LMC is generally managed by a certified media specialist and, depending on size, may have two or more professionals and additional clerical staff members. High school LMCs, which must meet the requirements of school accreditation from independent regional agencies, are most likely to fall into the category of integrated library media centers. Junior high school and middle school libraries fall predictably in between.

Some facilities are organized as combined school-public library facilities. The combined library facility is distinctive in its governance and funding. Where both policy and financial responsibility of similar institutions with differing missions are vested in a single infrastructure, there is opportunity for both conflict and effective operations. Savings in administration, management, and cooperative services are reasons given for the continuance of these arrangements. Small communities are well served by a single, accessible facility. The professional staff may have access to a larger support staff in combined facilities. Public library personnel may benefit financially if school employees are members of a teachers' union. Library professionals may be expected to possess credentials allowing them to work as both school and public librarians. In some cases, competition for collection development funds prevents the combined facility from reaching its full potential in programs, services, or collection goals.

FUNDING

Financial support for the library media program is one portion of the overall funding responsibility for education assumed by the local school district. The level of support local districts award school library media centers is a quantitative reflection of the district's educational philosophy. In most states budgetary decisions are made at the district level. Specific allocations for the library media program are often included in the overall budget for each building. Library media may or may not be a line item in the building budget when it comes from the district office. As a consequence, building-level budgetary decisions are ostensibly controlled by the building administrator.

Effective library media specialists assume an assertive role in becoming informed about the process for budget planning in their buildings and districts. Information about the time frame; budgetary system; state, regional, and local guidelines; and budgetary priorities is systematically gathered. The development of a budget proposal for the LMC that considers national standards, program goals, a quantitative inventory of the collection (in all media formats), users, and curriculum helps ensure that the media center's needs are an integral part of the decision process.

Special purpose grants are available in some states, particularly for networking, automation projects, and instructional technology products. Successful awards of such funding opportunities are often dependent upon careful monitoring of state board and legislative activities to identify available grants and awards and on the ability of the media specialist to complete a successful application. While the 1980s brought reductions in eligibility, funding levels, and accountability requirements, there are still federal supplemental funds for library media centers available through the School Improvement Act (1988).

There is increasing evidence that school library media specialists must become more astute in communicating the needs of the LMC to local administrators. School improvement goals and current funding climates provide a strong case for library media specialists to assume leadership roles in identifying and applying for outside public and private grants to support the library media program. The partnerships with local businesses and industry, being encouraged by the literature for all manner of educational needs, include support for the LMC. This trend will require the services of an increasingly sophisticated library media information specialist, attuned to effective managerial principles of organization and administration.

AUDIENCES

The school library media center serves a clearly identified user group. The public and private school teacher and learner, from kindergarten through the twelfth grade, constitute the primary audiences for the library media center. In recent years this traditional audience has been broadened to include the administrative staff, parents, and the preschool child.

Parents have traditionally been welcomed to the school library media center as participants in school and community service programs. Recently, they have become media center users in concert with innovative family literacy and parenting programs.

Preschool programs housed in public school buildings became common with the inception of the Headstart education movement in the 1960s. Programs and materials for preschool learners have only recently been considered on an equitable basis with materials funding and collection development goals for the traditional elementary school student. In the early years, school library media centers felt little responsibility for Headstart programs, whose funding often surpassed their own. Changes in Headstart program philosophy, structure, and funding, and education research that validates the importance of early structured learning activities for "at risk" children, have made it necessary to reevaluate services to this user group.

Innovative programs can be found that provide exposure to the library media center for preschoolers through storytimes and home circulation privileges, particularly in communities where alternative library services are unavailable.

SERVICES

The library media center is a planned, integrated concept that utilizes a combination of personnel, collection, funding, and facilities to provide a program characterized by managerial and operational functions, instructional goals, and resource materials expertise. Basic managerial services include:

- selection, ordering, processing, and organizing media and hardware for maximum access;

- development and implementation of policies and procedures for materials collection and center operations;

- assuming responsibility for maintenance of the collection and equipment; and

- public relations activities such as the observation of special library events, giving speeches and presentations to community groups, and publicizing media center materials and activities to promote the library media center program.

Services to learners include:

- providing reading, viewing, and listening guidance;

- providing structured instructional programs to teach information literacy and study skills, aesthetic appreciation of literature, and media production and presentation skills; and

- developing network relationships that provide information access beyond the center collection.

Basic services to teachers and administrators include:

- serving as a curriculum team member providing literature and information resource expertise, instructional design consultation, and grade/department level curriculum planning;

- providing leadership in the planning and implementation of professional development activities; and

- assisting in the preparation and execution of professional media presentation activities.

The library media program combines the concepts of a specialist with the competencies to function in each of the roles identified in *Information Power*, an on-site collection of instructional and recreational information resources, adequate technology for user access, and appropriate networking liaisons to facilitate information needs.

COLLECTIONS

The school library media collection has been defined in both specific and general terms by the standards documents that have driven library program development. With the exception of collection size and emerging material formats, there has been little change since the unified media concept was introduced in 1960. Current recommendations for collection sizes are based on the program variables of instructional goals and objectives, school enrollment, curriculum, learner needs and interests, and teaching methodologies. Both state guidelines and regional accreditation agencies provide quantitative measures for determining collection adequacy.

In contrast to the item-count approach that dominated evaluative measurement of the LMC in the past, current curriculum and instructional goals dictate a broad range of print and non-print media and hardware. Desirable collection scope includes media in every conceivable format, from traditional audiovisual and print formats to the new imaging, compact disc, and interactive media and developing delivery technologies. Also considered are materials that extend the collection beyond curriculum and instructional resources to include the personal information and leisure reading, viewing, and listening media that contribute to lifelong learning habits. This shift from quantitative to qualitative indexes is considered to be of greater import than the numerical measures produced by "standards."

The school library media center is expected to have a collection development policy that provides clearly articulated procedures for the selection and de-selection of materials. An outline of specific procedures for challenged materials, formally adopted by the local board of education, is a vital component of an effective collection policy.

PERSONNEL

The operational principle regarding personnel, as stated in *Information Power*, indicates: "All students, teachers, and administrators in each school building at all grade levels must have access to a library media program provided by one or more certificated library media specialist working full time in the school's library media center."[5]

Professional education for school media personnel has been addressed by the standards documents that have guided the progress of school library development. The dual issues of whether education for school librarianship should be provided at the undergraduate or graduate level and what master's level librarians should be called were hotly debated in the professional literature in the 1950s. In 1958, "the joint committee American Association of School Librarians — Association of College and Research Libraries — Department of Audio-Visual Instruction of the NEA defined the prerequisites for the attainment of professional status of instructional materials specialists."[6]

In 1967, at a conference co-sponsored by the ALA Office for Library Education and the Library Administrative Division, the issue of professional status was reintroduced, with conflicting conclusions. The end result was that education for school library media personnel at the paraprofessional, undergraduate, and master's levels was validated and continues to exist.[7]

The initial preparation program for the school library media specialist, as evidenced by library and information science education programs, clearly reflects the components identified by school library media professionals. It includes knowledge, skills, and competencies in the areas of library and information science, education, and communications theory and technology. The education component requires teacher certification, for which the responsibility is vested in the individual state boards of education. In many states one can receive a lifelong teaching certificate with only a bachelor's degree; neither the master's of library science nor a master of arts or science degree is needed. Consequently, the certification requirements for library media specialists differ from state to state. While several states require a master's in library science (MLS) degree, and all ALA-accredited library and information science schools offer the graduate professional degree, library education for school media personnel at the undergraduate level continues to be available in schools of education throughout the nation. This is so in some cases because salaries are very low or because teacher education is placed primarily at the undergraduate level. The operative thinking is that it is most logical to educate library media personnel at the same level as teachers, the undergraduate level. In states where certification guidelines have not, unequivocally, accepted the graduate level degree requirements indicated by the library profession, undergraduate programs train a substantial number of media personnel.

Accrediting agencies such as the North Central Association play an important role in library media staffing patterns by providing independent reviews of schools and colleges. These agencies recognized from the outset the importance of properly trained librarians and appropriate support staffing. Close monitoring, accompanied by formal protests by ALA and AASL of the tendency to lower library media standards (ofttimes based on pressures from conflicting professional standards), has resulted in clear and deliberate efforts by accrediting agencies to replicate the requirements identified by the library profession. North Central's 1990 accreditation guidelines call for a "qualified library media specialist" and appropriate support personnel, explicitly spelled out and tied to school enrollment figures.[8]

Library and information science schools that value the commendation that accompanies accredited status by their own profession submit their programs every seven years to a rigorous analytical review process from the ALA Committee on Accreditation (COA). The process includes goals and objectives that are reflected in the administration, governance, and curriculum; an intensive self-study evaluation; a visit from an outside team of peer reviewers; and analysis and evaluation of the school library media preparation program.

Schools of education located in universities and teacher education institutions are also subject to periodic reviews for the purpose of maintaining their accredited status. One of the largest accrediting agencies of schools of education is the National Committee for the Accreditation of Teacher Education (NCATE). In 1988 the NCATE Folio to prepare for accreditation visits listed ten areas in which school of education personnel must provide evidence of demonstrated competency in the preparation of school library media specialists. The competency areas were identified as:

1. Professional studies in teacher education, to provide an understanding of the principles and methods of teaching and learning and to prepare candidates who meet appropriate state certification requirements for teaching.

2. Professionalism: the ability to demonstrate a commitment to personal growth.

3. Communications and group dynamics.

4. Collection management: the application of basic principles of evaluation and selection to build and maintain a resource collection to support the educational goals of the school.

5. Collection management: for the support of the personal, developmental, and curricular needs of students and teachers.

6. Collection management: assisting faculty and students in the design and production of instructional resources.

7. Organization: the implementation and coordination of policies and procedures for efficient access to information and materials.

8. Administration: the implementation and coordination of policies and procedures for smooth management of personnel, resources, and facilities.

9. Instructional leadership: the provision of leadership and assistance to faculty and students in the teaching and learning process.

10. Access: the ability to develop a school library media program dedicated to providing access to information and ideas.

Library and information science schools have the option of choosing COA or NCATE accreditation, both, or neither. The choice is often determined by the parent university and the requirements and expectations of the job market.

Both *Media Programs: District and School* (1975) and *Information Power* (1988) provide strong arguments for the provision of support personnel in the LMC at all grade levels. Paraprofessionals functioning as media technicians, media aides, or clericals, in addition to volunteers and student assistants, are important elements in the successful implementation of the media program.

The availability of ESEA Title II funding in the 1960s facilitated the purchase of materials for library media programs across the country. The funding for staffing went, for the most part, to provide staff at the state level. A limited amount could be spent at the local level for acquisition and technical services functions. Consequently, most local level support personnel were placed in district level processing centers.

As full members of the teaching staff, library media specialists enjoy the same rights, privileges, responsibilities, compensation, and performance reviews that other members of the school community have. It remains an unfortunate fact that all children do not yet have equitable access to certified library media specialists in their schools. However, school library media specialists are the most prolific arm of the profession: there are more school library practitioners in the United States and Canada than any other type of information professional.

CONTEMPORARY ISSUES FOR SCHOOL MEDIA CENTERS

The 1988 guidelines for school library media programs, *Information Power*, embodies the principles identified by the library community in response to educational imperatives delivered in several reports on the state of public school education. "A Nation at Risk," (National Commission on Excellence in Education, 1983), "Tomorrow's Teachers: A Report of the Holmes Group" (1986), and *Schools of the Future: Education into the 21st Century* (1985) are three of the several searing critical treatises that were written in the 1980s. The regrettable failing among all three documents is the glaring omission of the role that libraries play as partners in the dissolution of barriers to providing quality education.

New perspectives about how instruction is delivered to the learner point to the importance of an instructional team approach to teaching methodologies. The ways in which media specialists can utilize "in place" knowledges, skills, and procedures are documented in *Information Power*. At issue is the fact that the paradigm shift in the philosophy of collection, scope, primary audience, and media program delivery systems does not emanate from a coalition of education societies and organizations. This newly articulated role represents the position of library media associate organizations alone. Soliciting consensus from other education organizations is central to the success of this new initiative.

Information Power charges the media specialist with providing in-depth curriculum and instructional methodology planning services to the classroom teacher as a member of the instructional team. Direct services to the teacher are viewed as an opportunity to provide a higher quality of service to learners.

While the provision of multimedia instructional materials that enhance teaching and address the instructional needs of all learners is not a new objective, curriculum planning with the media specialist as a full member of the instructional team, with responsibility for learning outcomes, represents a significant change. As a curriculum team consultant, the library media specialist identifies teaching strategies that utilize instructional materials most effectively. The overall intention to release the teacher from the restrictive bonds of textbook teaching through cooperative partnerships is the fundamental issue. The mandate to teach inquiry process and learning skills is key to the new paradigm.

Educational reform movements have centered on the potential role of the LMC to function as a true hub of the school. School improvement and restructuring plans provide an opportunity to redefine the library media program to foster informational and inquiry literacies that are necessary to function in the information-driven society of today and tomorrow.

The "whole language" and "literature-based" reading instruction education movements are learner-centered methodologies that require a full range of learning resources. The library media specialist is already positioned, by knowledge, education, and competency, to identify and provide access to these materials.

Nationally, district-by-district implementation of library media programs as conceived in *Information Power* and school improvement, restructuring, and school empowerment projects will require certified media specialists in numbers that far exceed the current rate of enrollment in library schools of students pursuing this specialty. This problem demands immediate attention from professional organizations, state education officials, and institutions of higher education with library media certification programs. The challenge it introduces is clearly multifaceted and will require a concentrated commitment from all sectors.

Funding priorities must be redirected to provide the support for equitable learner access to both print and electronic information resources. Aging collections, rising costs of books and periodicals, and requirements for capital investments in automation and technological hardware complicate the limited funding options available to school districts.

NOTES

[1] John T. Gillespie and Diana L. Spirt. *Administering the School Library Media Center* (New York: R. R. Bowker, 1983), pp. 2-17.

[2] Melvin M. Bowie. *Historic Documents of School Libraries* (Fayetteville, Ark.: Hi Willow Research & Publishing, 1986), p. 32.

[3] Gillespie and Spirt, *Administering*, p. 8.

[4] Ruth Ann Davies. *The School Library Media Center Program: A Force for Educational Excellence.* 2d ed. (New York: R. R. Bowker, 1974), p. 70.

[5] *Information Power: Guidelines for School Library Media Programs* (Chicago: American Library Association, 1988), p. 57.

[6] Davies, *School Library Media Center*, p. 70.

[7] American Library Association. *Library Needs and Utilization. Library Manpower Needs and Utilization*, ed. by Lester Asheim (Washington, D.C.: American Library Association, 1967), p. 35.

8 North Central Association of Colleges and Schools. *NCA Standards for Elementary, Middle Level, and Secondary Schools* (Tempe, Ariz.: Arizona State University and NCA Commission on Schools, 1990), pp. 17, 37, 46.

REFERENCE LIST

American Association of School Librarians. *Standards for School Library Programs.* Chicago: American Library Association, 1960.

American Association of School Librarians and Association for Educational Communications and Technology. *Media Programs: District and School.* Chicago: American Library Association, 1975.

American Association of School Librarians and Department of Audio-Visual Instruction. *Standards for School Media Programs.* Chicago: American Library Association, 1969.

American Association of School Librarians, School Library Manpower Project. *School Library Personnel Task Analysis Survey* (1969); *Occupational Definitions for School Library Media Personnel* (1971); *Behavioral Requirements Analysis Checklist* (1973); *Curriculum Alternatives: Experiments in School Library Media Education* (1974). Chicago: American Library Association.

American Library Association. *Library Needs and Utilization. Library Manpower Needs and Utilization.* Ed. by Lester Asheim. Conference Co-sponsored by the Office for Library Education and the Library Administration Division, March 9-11, 1967. Washington, D.C.: American Library Association, 1967.

Bowie, Melvin M. *Historic Documents of School Libraries.* Fayetteville, Ark.: Hi Willow Research & Publishing, 1986.

Cetron, Marvin. *Schools of the Future: Education into the 21st Century.* New York: McGraw-Hill, 1985.

Davies, Ruth Ann. *The School Library Media Center Programs.* 3d ed. New York: R. R. Bowker, 1979.

Holmes Group. "Tomorrow's Teachers: A Report of the Holmes Group." *Chronicle of Higher Education* 33 (November 26, 1986): 15-17.

Information Power: Guidelines for School Library Media Programs. Chicago: American Library Association, 1988.

Michigan Accreditation Program. Lansing, Mich.: Michigan State Board of Education, 1988.

Morris, Betty, John T. Gillespie, and Diana Spirt. *Administering the School Library Media Center*, 3d ed. New Providence, N.J.: R. R. Bowker, 1991.

National Commission on Excellence in Education. "A Nation at Risk: The Imperative for Education Reform." *Chronicle for Higher Education* 26 (May 4, 1983): 11-16.

Prostano, Emanuel T., and Joyce S. Prostano. *The School Library Media Center*. Littleton, Colo.: Libraries Unlimited, Inc., 1987.

Realities: Educational Reform in a Learning Society. Chicago: Task Force on Excellence in Education, American Library Association, 1984.

8

Types of Libraries and Information Centers: Special

DEFINITIONS, GOALS, AND OBJECTIVES

Of the many types of libraries that exist, no other is as difficult to define as the special library. There are actually many types of special libraries, with corresponding differences in the materials they stock and provide, the services they offer, and the clientele and demands they aim to satisfy. A special library is characteristically a unit or department of an organization that is primarily devoted to other than library or educational purposes. This definition is far from universal, however, for a special library may also refer to a subject department in a large public or academic library, or an independent library having no affiliation with any other institution.

The only unifying trait of all special libraries is that they are defined by the narrow scope of their services and collections. It is not their mission to serve a vast variety of interests, as a public library does, or to support curricular needs, as do academic or school libraries. Special libraries serve special purposes, which result in unique goals and objectives. Normally, they provide special materials to specialized clienteles. They tend to be small, contain relatively few materials when compared to most public or academic libraries, and employ few staff members, often because they are units of larger agencies or corporations. However, while their range and scope are small, their coverage is extensive, and, in some cases (e.g., presidential libraries), exhaustive.

One class of special libraries exists within corporations in the for-profit sector of the national economy. To stay alive and to justify their existences, special libraries in corporations must charge back services, showing a profit on all transactions. That this imperative may defeat or complicate the overriding directive of library service—to maximize service to the patron—is obvious.

Because a single definition covering all special libraries and information centers is impossible to formulate, a brief list of examples will serve to show the scope and variety of such agencies.

Objectives

Whereas objectives of academic, public, and school libraries are normally fairly consistent, those of special libraries, which exist in larger organizations, may vary greatly. If the parent institution is a business, seeking to make a profit and engaged in a competitive market, the mission and goals of the corporate library will be subject to the overall mission and goals of the company. Traditional library goals (of service to all, for example) often must be subordinate to business objectives (to maximize profitability and to outsell the competition). Increasingly, as academic institutions are being run more like businesses, more of such decision making may be seen in other types of libraries and information centers.

TYPES OF SPECIAL LIBRARIES

The following list is illustrative of the types of special libraries rather than comprehensive:

- society or association libraries

- medical libraries

- patient libraries in hospitals

- presidential libraries

- law libraries

- newspaper libraries

- libraries in corporations that produce food or drink

- museum libraries

- corporate headquarters libraries in multinational businesses

- military libraries

- prison libraries

- learned society libraries

- art institute libraries

- music libraries

- computer libraries

- patent libraries

- map libraries

- picture libraries

- church, synagogue, mosque, and other divinity libraries

Each of these may also be a collection within a more comprehensive library, such as the map collection or picture collection of an academic or public library.

Another unifying factor of most (yet not all) special libraries is that primary emphasis seems to be more on information than on format, which means that electronic databases and microform may be substituted for books as the primary storage and dissemination media.

THE SPECIAL LIBRARIAN/
INFORMATION SPECIALIST

What sort of person operates the special library? Normally, such a person, or at least the ideal candidate, has a strong and focused background in the subject or scholarly area that is the focus of the special library. The special librarian is usually in a considerably different position from the generalist, being first an employee of the parent organization or company and only secondarily a librarian. Yet here is one of the most vexing issues facing special librarians. The information profession feels that its members have a first obligation to the information and the clients and only a secondary responsibility to the corporation and its "bottom line." Services in special libraries, however, are geared more to organizational needs than to the social betterment of the general public or of society.

Because the clienteles are restricted in most special libraries (although special departments and special collections within more general libraries are another matter), the services rendered have a narrow focus. Frequently the ability to make constructive use of such a library facility requires that the user possess some specialized or advanced knowledge of the subject matter. A special library is normally organized for quick and efficient access, and in serving that end may have its own, situation-specific classification system and style of shelf arrangement.

Consider the case of a worker in a scientific, technological, or industrial setting, for example, a research chemist in a pharmaceutical firm that produces several product lines of over-the-counter and prescription pain-killers. In the general fields of chemistry and biology, both of which must be considered for successful drug production, it is estimated that a paper is published somewhere in the world approximately every two minutes. Even if one *could* corral and assemble all those papers, reading them for comprehension would not be possible. Many would be in foreign languages, others would turn out to be unrelated to the particular research interest, and still others would be inaccessible.

Also, an employer does not normally pay its employees to read. Librarians, indexers, and preparers of abstracting services may be paid to read, in a sense, but this individual is a chemist, paid to make, refine, and test the company's products. He might work in a laboratory environment, mixing chemicals, testing them in various ways, and evaluating results. Suppose that the employer is enlightened enough to realize that professional reading is important to successful research in pharmaceutical chemistry. Suppose further that the company allowed him two hours per day to read from the literature of the subject area, to see what competitors and colleagues are doing, to keep up on developments, trends, experiments, and ongoing work in the field. The underlying assumption behind a voluntary reduction of lab time by one-quarter is that the employee learns at least enough in the time relinquished from the lab schedule to compensate his employer for time lost.

Even if he could spend two hours a day, five days a week, reading on company time, by the end of the first year of reading, the employee would be up to ten years behind the cutting edge of rapidly developing technology. So is there any viable way out of the dilemma of not being able to tackle all that reading but still needing to acquit oneself adequately in the workplace?

It is the job of the special librarian in this type of library to attempt to take on the enormous mountain of literature of potential value to the company's projects and products and to boil it down to more manageable proportions, much as important executives have various levels of secretarial help to sift through the people who seek to lay claim to their time.

How does this person perform such a miracle on a daily basis?

The special librarian acquires, through subscription, order, or direct purchase, a great variety of materials that potentially could be of use to the persons in the library's principal audience. A unique situation exists in that, unlike that of other types of libraries, the clientele of some special libraries is identified. The librarians know who they are and, by profiling, interview, and questionnaire, they have a general idea of what the users want to read and with what priorities and limitations they must work.

This special librarian would use a specific profile that could not be used by librarians in other types of special libraries. It is possible (and generally desirable) to design a survey instrument that will present a number of choices to the chemist so that he may check the specific subjects or topical areas of primary and secondary interest to him simply by placing a check or double-check in the box next to the designated areas of interest. Once the profiles from various employees are submitted and collated (which may be a useful computer function), the special librarian has a reasonable idea both of what will be of potential interest to specific individuals and, perhaps more important, of what will not. In this way, only materials that appear to be relevant to one's research interests will be routed selectively to that individual's workstation.

Psychologically, it is highly desirable to reduce the amount of literature awaiting one's attention because people like their information in drips, not clumps, and there is something daunting about piles of *anything* awaiting action, whatever the nature of the material.

To make it possible for the research chemist to have only a manageable (low recall) stack of assumed high-precision (relevant) material before him, several prior operations must take place. A special librarian must either know and understand the individual, or have access to a copy of that person's research interests profile. Alternatively, the librarian may examine each new piece of information to establish what it is about and only *then* attempt to worry about whom it might concern or interest.

The special librarian is engaged in *active* librarianship, reading and evaluating each item with a known population of users in mind, and with a view to trying to get the right information to the right persons at the right time, delivered to their desks or computer mailboxes in a way that saves time and maximizes utilization.

Among the many daily tasks of the typical special librarian are some that raise issues for the information professional:

- In homegrown indexing, how can the librarian perform subject assignment so that documents will be "marked and parked" for ready retrieval by various corporate employees?

- How should the librarian profile employees to achieve a reasonable idea of how to determine who should get what?

- Is it possible to perform selective dissemination of information, based on previously stored profiles, for a large number of demanding clients, so that as little important material as possible slips by unnoticed?

- How can materials (in various formats) be routed selectively to offices, desks, or electronic mailboxes of employees who are judged to get the most from them? Remember that a document inappropriate for a particular reader wastes time, while failing to call a document to the attention of a reader who could profit from it wastes money and retards growth.

- Is it possible to write abstracts of documents so that readers can tell after perusing a scant hundred words whether they think they need to read the entire work?

- Can a homegrown and home-maintained corporate index of subject terms to the necessary levels of specificity take the place of a thesaurus prepared for a general class of libraries or users?

- Can publication lag and time lag be overcome to route information necessary to effective job performance without delay to those readers who might use it best?

- How can librarians in special environments best perform reference service, both on demand and without waiting to be asked, without being intrusive or disruptive?

- How often must library staff monitor and update user profiles to accommodate new interests or changes in focus?

- Since many important documents in science are in languages other than English, and chemists in this country are not presumed to read in foreign languages, how can information staff arrange for rapid, accurate translation without incurring great expense?

Special libraries do not all extend their services at the same levels. Three levels of specificity — minimal, intermediate, and maximal — can be said to represent the degrees of activist librarianship. At the minimal level, a range of services is performed for the user *on demand*, meaning that the librarian provides information and assistance when asked, pretty much as is done in public and academic libraries. At the intermediate level, a degree of effort is made to alert members of the clientele to the existence and availability of information and documents in their profile areas, but such effort is not the highest priority among the librarian's tasks. At the maximal level (which requires a great deal of staff time and therefore, money), staff so acquaint themselves with the desires and needs of members of their audience that they scrutinize each new item with specific people in mind, route items selectively to those they think may best put them to use, and (sometimes) translate documents, or track them down, frequently hand-carrying them into the presence of the user, also providing commentary.

An interesting question arises here: Who makes the best special librarian in such a research and development (R & D) setting, the practitioner, who knows the subject specialty well, or the reference librarian, who is generally well versed in information-finding techniques yet has no particular subject knowledge prior to employment? In some situations, a person with no technical background would be lost, but on the other hand, the corporation wants a skilled and amicable "people-person" to help employees find information, not to do the analysis itself. Clearly, *both* traits are desired in the same individual, but if one must choose, which is preferable?

Another general question worth thinking about is whether it is better in a special library setting to teach people how to use information or just to give them the information. Normally, there are advantages to either policy. When you show people how to find information, they presumably have learned enough to make optimal use of a library to find their own information in the future. The downside of this is that they must spend (waste?) their valuable time in searching out materials, when a competent special librarian could find it faster and better. The other policy, that of *giving* people information, may work better in a special setting, but it deprives users of the rudimentary skills they need subsequently to find things out for themselves.

CONTEMPORARY ISSUES FOR SPECIAL LIBRARIES

Automation

The vaunted advantage of automation is that it saves time through efficiency, returning much for a minimal effort; time, for special libraries and information centers more than for any other type of library, is literally money. Yet this is not the case always and everywhere. Also, there is some question whether the money expended on automation is worth the enhanced capabilities when it might be equally well spent on, for example, extra periodical subscriptions. Whether we welcome automation in libraries or view it with alarm or caution (and there is still room for both attitudes), it is here to stay, and rather than fighting it we must find ways to turn its capabilities to our advantage.

Organization

When the profit motive is present it is especially important that a special library be set up in such a way as to maximize operational efficiency. Ideally, therefore, all efforts should be coordinated to see to it that each member of the special library's audience of patrons receives what he (and *only* what he) needs, boiled down to manageable proportions and delivered in a timely fashion to his workstation. How best to achieve this dream is not merely a matter of money: it involves careful observation, close attention to feedback from the audience, time, energy, and planning.

Personnel

Not everyone who receives the master's degree in library and information science can become an effective special librarian. Nor can everyone who acts as an effective special librarian be equally competent in another type of information agency. First among qualities and skills most prized in such a professional is a strong and current subject background in the library's primary focus area. Another important trait is a mixture of assertiveness and a strong service orientation. In the special library setting, it is of first importance for the information specialist to anticipate and elicit the nature of the information required. The special librarian, especially in a corporate setting, must actively and assertively convey information to the patron, based upon a fairly thorough knowledge of what that patron wants, needs, and will find useful. For this reason, the special librarian must work closely, person-to-person, with those he serves, which admittedly is not everybody's cup of tea.

Job Security

In many library/information work settings, an employee receives a more or less permanent offer of employment upon completing a probationary period during which his performance is observed and evaluated. Rarely is job security such an issue as it is in a corporate environment, where a single individual at the highest corporate level can eliminate a librarian's job, a whole department, or an entire division of a large corporation. In today's uncertain economic times, such a scenario may well exist in all library settings, but the corporate sphere of operations is the one in which arbitrary decisions affecting librarians' jobs are most prevalant.

Education and Training

The profit motive, so important to a corporate enterprise, makes a big difference in what the mission, functions, and tasks of special librarians are, especially as compared to those of librarians in other roles. Idiosyncratic methods, policies, and procedures occur in special libraries more than in any other type of library setting. The procedures one might have learned in library school or on other jobs don't necessarily obtain on the job at hand: the employer will dictate methods, and decisions are normally made on the basis of what is likely to make the most money for the parent corporation. Any academic course for the training of special librarians must incorporate this diversity of practice. Special librarians exist in many disparate settings and accomplish many divergent purposes. In special libraries, therefore, on-the-job training becomes extremely important, as staff members must learn not so much *how* to do the job of the special librarian as *how to do it in a particular way* for a particular group of patrons.

None of this is to suggest that corporate executives don't or won't welcome suggestions, change, or departures from established rules. But most corporate librarians are obliged to think like corporate team members first and like librarians second. For this and other reasons, training works best when it is on-the-job, for few special librarians find that they can take the things they learned in school or at one job and use them without change at the next job.

Special librarians, perhaps more than others, are feeling a number of pressures on their ability to perform their assigned tasks with optimal effectiveness. These pressures translate into issues:

- As previously mentioned, the short and ever-decreasing "doubling time" for the amount of information in existence keeps aggravating the problem of bibliographic control.

- More formats for information are available. The days when librarians could concentrate on print sources for information are long departed.

- Technical information used by special libraries is accelerating at a geometric rate, although it would probably be unwise to equate the growth of information with that of knowledge.

- Technology contributes much to the ability to access information rapidly and precisely, but also contributes a set of problems of potentially serious nature to the conundrum of serving users better.

- The emphasis in special libraries has changed through the years from ownership or availability of information to delivery, intended to save the time and labor of the users, thus benefiting the parent concern.

- Changing user expectations and increasingly competitive corporate environments have placed pressure on special libraries to be even more responsive to user needs than they were previously.

- It is less important, thanks to telecommunications and electronic mail, for users physically to enter special libraries nowadays. Distance is technically irrelevant, and the employees in Europe and Asia of a corporation based in the United States have almost the same ease of access to information as the workers just down the hall. This permits special librarians to concentrate on improved methods of getting information around to user workstations, regardless of location, with a minimal time lag and at reasonable cost.

- Competing demands on staff time have made it important that time spent in serving user needs be used wisely and well.

- The desirability of a transparent (i.e., as invisible as possible) user interface calls for new ways of handling requests for information. The important concern is with getting information and answers to questions into the hands (and minds) of users without making them aware of the problems of the librarians. New electronic interfaces will cause problems for those corporate users who feel a degree of technophobia. Newer employees will come to their jobs with these skills in place and training programs can assist most of the rest. For most employees, however, a human intermediary on call to provide advice or assistance or to perform searches will still be welcomed.

More sophisticated corporate users can now search the total information system without demanding the attention of an overworked (and sometimes frazzled) library staff member and without any possible interpersonal glitches in communication. Some of the special library's clientele will become adept at finding their own information (an opportunity not always the case in public and academic library settings), which will have the beneficial effect of freeing library staff members to assist those who genuinely need help.

Special libraries, by definition, tend to have less in common with one another than other types of libraries do. Each is a part of something larger. Each special librarian must try to serve the ends and goals of the corporate enterprise while attempting to do the work of information acquisition, organization, and dissemination traditionally associated with the profession. However, special librarians' assertive, activist stance with regard to patron desires and needs may well be a preview of the future of libraries in all sorts of environments. Nothing is more inspirational to our profession than a library staff so dedicated to serving its clientele that it will do almost anything to put the right information into the right hands at the right time. And special librarians, especially those in the for-profit sector, are (or should be) most highly motivated to perform that task.

REFERENCE LIST

Drake, Miriam A. "Information Management and Special Librarianship." *Special Libraries* 73 (October 1982): 225-37.

Guide to Career Opportunities for Special Librarians and Information Professionals. Washington, D.C.: Special Libraries Association, 1987.

Mount, Ellis. *Special Libraries and Information Centers: An Introductory Text.* New York: Special Libraries Association, 1983.

"Objectives and Standards for Special Libraries." *Special Libraries* 65 (December 1964): 671-80.

Tees, Miriam. "Graduate Education for Special Libraries: What Special Librarians are Looking for in Graduates." *Special Libraries* 77 (Fall 1986): 190-97.

Thury, Eva M. "From Library to Information Center: Case Studies in the Evolution of Corporate Information Resources." *Special Libraries* 79 (Winter 1988): 21-27.

Waldron, Helen J. "The Business of Running a Special Library." In Jackson, Eugene B., ed., *Special Librarianship: A New Reader*, pp. 142-50. Metuchen, N.J.: Scarecrow Press, 1980.

White, Herbert S. "What Are Special Libraries and Information Centers?" In *Managing the Special Library: Strategies for Success within the Larger Organization*, pp. 1-12. White Plains, N.Y.: Knowledge Industry Publications, 1984.

Wood, Bill M. "The Special Library Concept of Service." *American Libraries* 3 (1972): 759-68.

Zachert, Martha Jane, and Robert V. Williams. "Marketing Measures for Information Services." *Special Libraries* 77 (Winter 1986): 61-70.

9 Contemporary Issues of Public Service and Policy

ACCESS TO INFORMATION

The Freedom of Information Act (FOIA) is intended to provide free access to information of all types held in or by governmental agencies, particularly those of the United States federal government. Professional librarians are primarily concerned with public access to information, and it is understandable, therefore, that they act to provide free access to information to all persons, without regard to ability to pay or status in society. In practice, however, there are varying degrees of free access to information. The definition of the word *free* is also open to interpretation; does free mean without charge, or merely without restrictions ... or both?

Provision of free information, however, does not necessarily mean that anyone may have access to anything held in any of the federal government's repositories of information. There are nine specific exemptions intentionally built into the FOIA:

1. Legitimately "classified" information (e.g., "top secret" documents).

2. Internal personnel rules and practices.

3. Information specifically exempted by other statutes.

4. Trade secrets and privileged commercial information.

5. Inter- or intra-agency memoranda that embody the agency's deliberative process.

6. Personnel and medical files.

7. Investigative reports compiled for law enforcement purposes (but there are exceptions to this exception).

8. Audit files prepared for regulation of banks and other financial institutions.

9. Geological data concerning wells.

When library professionals become involved in trying to gain access to such information, they will normally discover that access is denied. Beyond these more-or-less clearly delineated exceptions, however, the public is supposed to have access to government-supplied or government-held information.

PRIVATIZATION OF INFORMATION

A *New York Times* article from February 21, 1989 explained that librarians were protesting a proposal that would take the government out of the business of interpreting and organizing some of its computer information. Under the new regulation, federal agencies would continue to issue data, but they would not translate the material into charts, graphs, and analyses if such a service is available through private sources for a fee. Librarians fear that this proposal by the Office of Management and Budget would make government information costs higher than the relatively modest fees now charged by public information utilities for providing materials. The outcome of this may be that those without sufficient financial resources will be effectively disenfranchised, cut off from the information they want or need, because they lack the money to pay for it.

The American Library Association has passed a resolution urging Congress to guarantee ready access to all requestors of computerized federal information without regard to financial wherewithal. Without some action, society's "have-nots" would, for economic reasons alone, be unable to gain access to or secure the information they need. Such moves serve only to exacerbate the existing and growing problem of the gap between the haves and the have-nots (in a new sense of "information-rich" and "information-poor"). The government, however, defends its move by claiming that such action will serve to increase (rather than diminish) access to government information, by letting private concerns market and supply the material needed, while releasing the government from the obligation to retain and supply so many documents.

AUTOMATION OF LIBRARY SERVICES

It is a futile argument to debate automation in the 1990s, since it already has such a pronounced hold on the library community and promises to become more pervasive during the last years of the century. However, there is value in taking an analytical look at automation, to assess its universality for all processes and services in the information-provision field.

Automation of library services was once thought of as a visionary concept. Today, and increasingly, automation isn't just on its way; it's here. The question, therefore, becomes not whether, but when. In 1971, Ellsworth Mason, an academic librarian, expounded his negative view of the virtues of library automation in *Library Journal*. After some months of studying the cost/benefit economics of automating library operations, he concluded that:

My observation convinced me that the computer is not for library use; that all promises offered in its name are completely fraudulent; that not only is it extremely expensive compared to other methods at this time, but that it will become increasingly expensive in the future; that it has been wrapped so completely in an aura of unreason that fine intelligences are completely uprooted when talking about it; that its use in a library weakens the library as a whole by draining off large sums of money for a small return; and that it should be stamped out.[2]

Even twenty years ago, Mason was in the minority, as he strove valiantly to stem the tide of enthusiasm for computerizing academic libraries. It must also be pointed out that much has changed in two decades and that today's computers are vastly more powerful; their software is improved and more capable; their costs have either held steady or, in numerous cases, decreased; and their reliability has improved in many ways.

Still, Mason is only one of a considerable chorus of voices warning or asking us to take a long, hard, objective look at computers and what they can do when measured against other, more conventional, manual systems, before pronouncing computerization of library operations an unqualified success. Most academic libraries, especially the larger ones, need not worry about *whether* to automate. Automation is in evidence in most areas; now we must figure out how to make it more sophisticated and more responsive to the needs of patrons. Costs also are a concern. Even though today's dollar goes somewhat further in terms of how much automation equipment it will buy, there is still the salient point that the money spent on computerizing the library cannot be spent on books, periodicals, and other materials.

Thomas Ballard, a public librarian, is a current version of Mason, which shows that there will always be skeptics, detractors, and critics of automation. Ballard's prime concern is that, based on studies he has conducted, "people," by which he means the library-using public, don't want gleaming new contraptions of metal and plastic for their library tax dollar nearly as much as they want books. More books, more copies of current best-sellers, more titles to choose from, and more printed periodical and newspaper subscriptions are what people come to libraries for, and Ballard is willing to put to the test the myth of the computer as a panacea for library problems. The most people-pleasing move in the long run is just to load up on new titles and forget about mortgaging our libraries' futures to companies offering automated systems, at least until the bugs are worked out of the machines, which seem to become obsolete as fast as they are installed.[3] Such concerns apply equally to academic, special, and even school libraries, and few problems of automation are restricted to one type of library or information center.

TECHNOPHOBIA

Technophobia refers to the irrational and extreme fear that some persons develop when confronted with technological progress. In the popular parlance, it stands for fear of computers; sometimes it can result in lost or restructured careers and millions of dollars lost or misspent each year because employees cannot or will not learn to deal with the machines.

Human beings vary considerably in their ability to adapt to changes in the environment. Some seem able to embrace new concepts and procedures readily, making transitions without apparent effort. Others are shocked by change and become threatened, numbed, combative, or mocking towards change, agents and implements of change, and those who propound them. It should come as no surprise, therefore, that library automation is greeted with a complete spectrum of reactions, ranging from fear and loathing to enthusiastic, sometimes even reckless, acceptance.

A portion of each library staff and a percentage of the people in any community will not welcome computers. Frequently one hears remarks to the effect that staff members didn't come into librarianship to become slaves to machines; most professional librarians entered the field because of the earnest desire to be around books *and* people and to have the opportunity (in the Boolean sense) to bring them together for mutual benefit. The public is divided on whether computers are necessary or even desirable in modern life and people differ in their ability and willingness to cope with such new-fangled devices as online catalog terminals. On the other hand, card catalogs were never all that easy for the average person to fathom; some average people, having fathomed them, say "nuts" to both the old and new technologies. Why should we expect any sort of easy familiarity with online catalogs?

David Kaser tells a story about the historic and chronic distress of technophobia.[4] When printing from movable metal type spread throughout Europe and ordinary citizens were able to purchase and own books, numerous nobles and landed gentry of various countries declined the temptation to acquire such books. These ubiquitous newfangled, and, to some minds, cheapjack products of runaway technology were so vastly inferior to the traditional, time-honored, handcrafted books that many prospective purchasers would have been ashamed or affronted to have them in their homes or libraries. But, says Kaser, do you know what happened to all those fifteenth- and sixteenth-century people who so passionately decried, defied, and resisted the new technology? They died. And with them died the resistance, and new generations of readers were born who did not know that there was anything cheap and common about printed books, readers who didn't have the same veneration for manuscripts (although they might have admired the craftmanship).

Time passed, and today virtually every book in private hands or public or academic libraries (excluding a few special collections) has been printed or otherwise reproduced by machine.

The point of this story is made in other terms by Marshall McLuhan, the late Canadian professor of humanities, who said that in every age there have been (and are going to be) many people who fear or even loathe progress, because it represents change and it is safer to stay where one is, not daring or risking the transition to the unfamiliar.[5] Eventually, rebellion or refusal to countenance the new becomes resignation in some and familiarity in the rest. When the public realizes the benefits of the new technology, the hardliners are forced to acquiesce, gracefully or otherwise, while the vanguard rushes forward to embrace the new. So even those who are presently in the rejectionist camp of library workers or users will give way eventually to a new breed who accepts automation technology as a natural part of life and would actually feel lost without it.

The implications of this process for library managers who are confronted (literally) by staff who don't approve of computers and by patrons who just can't seem to get used to online catalog terminals are that waiting out this transitional stage will bring rewards and that successive generations will react less negatively and exhibit more approval for the application of technology to the solution of library problems. The small but vocal percentage of staff members who can't or won't cope with computerization of traditional processes may have to seek other forms of employment.

I & R, ADVOCACY, AND ADVICE

I & R (information and referral) was spawned in public libraries whose staffs felt that they were simply being too passive to fulfill their missions and sought to provide not just information and materials, but *help*. How does I & R differ from ordinary reference service? I & R is generally concerned with helping citizens cope with the questions and problems of daily living, providing up-to-date information on the services of thousands of community organizations. I & R has many claimants to parenthood, but it is enough to say that some 30 years ago it was an idea whose time had come. At that time, libraries began experimenting with creating offshoots of their reference services to deal with common, everyday problems of life and to attempt to make people aware that their tax-supported libraries were ready, willing, and able to assist them with acquiring the things they wanted or needed or with coping with problems. I & R services, which varied (and still do) widely with the library, included consumer information; suicide, drug, gay, and alcohol counseling referral; entitlement programs information and registration; voter issues information, consumer complaint assistance; and translation into or from foreign languages.

The problems engendered by I & R were as considerable and impressive as were the potential benefits. For example, there are a number of problems involved with advocacy. How far should a library go in providing "help" to a patron if there was another interest working contrary to the patron's own? Rephrasing the question, to what extent was advocacy (in the sense of acting as attorney, social worker, ombudsman, etc.) on behalf of one client or patron advisable, proper, or safe for a public library that existed putatively to serve *all* its clientele? Do librarians really want or think it right to come between two warring parties, or to support one little person with a grievance in fighting city hall or the state or federal government? Embarking on these relatively uncharted waters of protocol and permissibility was considered risky at best.

I & R had its beginnings in the early 1960s in England, when British Citizens Advice Bureaus became common in larger cities. These bureaus were independent of libraries, however, and it was not until the idea was imported to the United States that the notion of incorporating I & R into public libraries was realized in the Enoch Pratt Free Library in Baltimore. Early attempts to justify I & R met with general failure and the services were stopped after four less-than-successful years. In 1971, the Detroit Public Library assembled files and trained staff for a somewhat different incarnation of the same idea, to be called TIP (The Information Place). Faced with massive budget cuts, the library administration hoped that "community information" would be one way of demonstrating the library's impact on the city's citizens, thus preventing further reductions in staff, hours, materials, etc. Unlike Pratt, Detroit integrated TIP with regular library services, and a large-scale publicity campaign helped advertise the new service. In the next decade, numerous city libraries opened I & R services, despite critics who pointed out that TIP was riding (or even crossing) the fine line between library service and social work.

At some levels, depending on philosophy as much as budget, the library's I & R service merely provides referral in the form of telephone numbers or names to ask for. At higher levels, the I & R service may either put the requester in direct contact with pertinent individuals or services or actually make calls or visits on the patron's behalf. At the highest level, the library staff offers to pick up, accompany, and drop off the questioner, providing assistance or interpretation as needed.

Some examples of the problems with which public library I & R services have dealt successfully are abandoned houses, community organizing for action, government services and entitlements, health care, landlord-tenant disputes, marriage counseling, mental health referrals, runaways, senior citizen housing, suicide prevention, welfare eligibility, women's organizations, and zoning appeals.

Normally, the I & R staff members who represent their library strive for neutrality, despite their personal attitudes, preferences, and predilections. But it is not always possible to provide information and/or referral on such "hot" topics as the ones listed above without either becoming involved or appearing to become involved in the client's struggle. In library schools, librarians receive conflicting messages from the faculty members. On the one hand, librarians are taught the importance of endorsing and "living" the Library Bill of Rights, which advocates "balance" in collections and non-judgmental stances in selection of materials for heterogeneous communities of readers/users. Does this, in itself, mean that the library, or its staff, normally do not take a stand for or against anyone or anything? Must the professional remain neutral in the face of unfairness, injustice, squalor, indifference, racism, etc.? It sometimes seems that there are only two choices: caring and not caring. This is one of the agonizing dilemmas of any library or library professional attempting to organize and run an I & R service. How far do we carry the notion of advocacy? Have we abandoned our moral high ground when we declare ourselves to be champions of those we represent? What adverse consequences can ensue from being cast as "attorneys" for our clients, and does this constitute practicing law without a license? Isn't it safer to stick with the skillful provision of facts, documents, names, and numbers? Each library must wrestle with these issues and choose its stance.

FEE-BASED SERVICES

It is a commendable notion that libraries are, and ought to be, forever free of direct costs to their patrons. After all, even the most nominal charge or fee imposes a barrier between those who are able to pay and those who are not, a condition which goes against democratic principles and underscores the contention of numerous social critics that the gap between the haves and the have-nots is real and widening. It is, however, a visionary and unrealistic notion that, when taxes pay for a library to exist and be stocked with materials, that library must become a source of all the materials, information, and services needed for the satisfaction of the public's entire range of information and recreational needs. Therefore, the "free versus fee" issue is now a matter of passionate debate. Should charges and costs be passed along to the users, or should the library depend only upon other allocations to finance provision of goods and services?

This issue inspires passions in those who must deal with it. Few are neutral, although most of us can see good points on both sides. One position is that since users have already paid for their library service through taxation, tuition, school millages, etc., it is both unfair and wrong to require or expect that they will pay again through user fees or charges. The classic position is that publicly supported libraries should be "free" in every sense. A more practical point is that charges and fees drive away customers, and, further, that librarians, by instituting systems of extra charges, are only helping to intensify and accelerate the economic gap between society's haves and have-nots. Opponents of fee charging fear that the eventual result of such practices could be effective disenfranchisement of the poor.

Among the more common charges and fees for information and non-information goods and services already in existence in America's libraries or being contemplated are:

- community resident renewable annual card (for a public library)

- non-community resident annual card

- admission charges (to programs, film showings, etc.)

- photocopying

- online searching

- per-item charges for borrowing materials (e.g., rental books, videos, computer games)

- research service

- reference question charges

- reserve cards

- overdue fines

- interlibrary loan fees

- sale of merchandise (e.g., cups, banners, posters)

- food service, coffee, etc.

- tool and equipment rental (e.g., power tools, appliances)

- non-resident differential on various services.

Those who oppose fees for library services want library admission and use to be free of direct costs, so that any person may enter and take advantage of the library without having or spending any money. The reasons are twofold: (1) the governing body for the library should provide adequate funding so that no additional fees, charges, or other revenues are necessary and (2) users are already paying (in one way or another) for library services, whether they use them or not, and it is unfair to require those who use the library to pay twice.

Some states (e.g., Connecticut, Michigan) are developing or already have in place statewide public library cards, which make borrowing possible at all participating member libraries. While this scheme may seem meritorious, critics point out the unfairness of expecting local citizens to provide, through their tax assessment, free service to persons who do not reside and pay taxes in that jurisdiction. As this case makes clear, easy solutions to the "free versus fee" controversy are impossible to attain. Someone will always feel exploited, overburdened, undercompensated, or powerless to avoid expenses that seem unfair.

COMMUNITY ANALYSIS AND LIBRARY SELECTION POLICIES

A good and universal maxim for library practitioners to follow is "know your community," words which apply equally to public, academic, school, and special libraries. There are numerous ways in which librarians may seek to know their communities, but they are all designed to permit the library better to serve its audience. *Community analysis* refers to the process by which one may study the community that has an impact on the library agency, describing its traits and personality, measuring the community's degree of participation in and need for library services, and judging the library's response and effectiveness at accomplishing the goals it has set for itself with respect to that community.

Naturally this procedure should be carried out in a reasonably systematic way. The first item that should exist before the library undertakes a community analysis is a selection and materials policy. Such a policy should be clearly stated and should explain comprehensibly what types of material the library will buy, and why, and what, if anything, the library will not provide, and why not.

CENSORSHIP AND INTELLECTUAL FREEDOM

Entire books and innumerable articles have been written on the important subject of censorship and intellectual freedom. This topic is among the most common and passionately argued in library literature. This discussion touches on the highlights only. A few informal working definitions are provided here. *Censorship*, in the library context, is the power to forbid, suppress, remove, refuse to add, label, store in a remote area, or place off limits any of the library's materials.

Intellectual freedom, broadly, means that people in a pluralistic society have both the freedom and the right to think as they like and say what they please, without governmental interference, except where "clear and present danger" to others is possible. For example, it has never been permissible to holler "fire!" as a joke in a crowded theater; most legal scholars agree that there are some sensible exclusions and exceptions to the absolute right of expression. Citizens in a free society generally expect that they will be able to find and have access to information or materials on any topic of inquiry without official or unofficial censorship impeding their search.

Obscenity is a term that is used these days with considerable impunity and is often confused with *indecency*, which is so subjective as to defy definition completely. In the popular sense, *obscene* refers to that which is disgusting, repulsive, vile, offensive, or loathsome, which is always a matter of opinion. And while no necessary connection exists between the obscene and the sexual, society tends to link them together. According to *The Encyclopedia of Crime and Justice* (New York: The Free Press, 1983), something may be obscene without having anything to do with sex at all, while the discussion or display of sex may be deemed artistic expression or erotic realism without being obscene.

Pornography, in its strict sense, is the portrayal of sexual activity. Contemporary interpretation by judicial bodies confines pornography to the somewhat narrow instance of portrayals designed to produce sexual arousal. Pornography need not be obscene, unless one subscribes to the notion that any portrayal or description of sex is inherently disgusting. Legal usage has done much to obliterate the distinction between obscenity and pornography. It is generally stipulated that pornography is obscene, with or without evidence, due procedure, or proof.

The current operational definition of obscenity in the United States proceeds from the *Miller vs. the United States* (1973) decision. Simply stated, a work (not necessarily a book) is obscene if it meets three criteria (and it must meet all three):

1. To the average person, applying contemporary community standards, and taken as a whole, it must predominantly appeal to a prurient interest in nudity, sex, or excretion;

2. taken as a whole, it must lack serious literary, artistic, political, or scientific value; and

3. it must depict or describe, in a patently offensive way, sexual conduct (listed in the decision).

A moment's reflection makes it clear that under these criteria few books would be considered "obscene." And while that is gratifying to most proponents of intellectual freedom, it alarms and offends other members of American society.

As this book is being written, several states have court cases in preparation which, if decided against intellectual freedom, will be referred to the United States Supreme Court with a view to overturning *Miller*. The newly reconstituted Court, with its pronounced rightward shift, may rule in favor of replacing *Miller*, with an "easier" test of obscenity in literature or the performing or visual arts, so that more works become legally obscene and therefore prohibited.

While censorship in American society focuses on sexual content, there is plenty of effort to restrict, remove, or ban materials from libraries, bookstores, and video parlors based upon their treatment of religion, minorities, political views, or family values.

The reader is invited to consider carefully the implications of censorship for who may read what. Such concerns may be translated into the following questions for information professionals:

- What are the cultural bases of censorship? Do some citizens know better than others what is "right" to read? Are they immune to adverse effects if they read these things themselves?

- Is restraint on the freedom to read necessary? What might happen if it were absent?

- What evidence is there to prove that a link exists between reading/viewing/listening and subsequent behavior?

- Does the innocence of children (the most frequently given reason for censorship) need protecting? If so, up to what age, and based on what criteria?

- Who should be empowered to limit intellectual freedom, assuming that someone must do it? (Government, religious groups, citizens groups, law enforcement agencies, teachers, and individual parents all seek to wear this mantle.)

- Should public opinion be the basis of any censorship measures, or may we tust government and the clergy to take care of this matter?

This book assumes that the reader is committed to preserving the basis of intellectual freedom: the right to read, view, hear, and experience what is available without interference from others. Nevertheless, a series of issues arises as to how best to combat attempts to censor library materials or to restrict their availability:

- Must information professionals strictly uphold such documents as the Librarian's Code of Ethics and a Code of Ethics for Information Scientists (see Appendixes A and B), even if they sometimes are at variance with our own beliefs and actions?

- How should librarians prepare lines of defense in anticipation of challenges from individual citizens and pressure groups before they occur?

- Which organizations, groups, media, and individuals are potential allies in the struggle against censorship and likely to join or form coalition groups in support of intellectual freedom or to write or broadcast editorials on the library's behalf?

- What is the best way to familiarize library workers with federal, state, and local legislation pertaining to censorship?

- What should the library's materials selection policy say about intellectual freedom, censorship, and selection?

- Who should have the ultimate authority and criteria for selection?

- What procedures should be followed when library material is challenged?

- What steps can be taken to ensure confidentiality of user records?

Despite the proven efficacy of preparation and strategy in combating censorship in the community, you may sometimes lose a fight. Be prepared to continue the struggle. Remember that the long-range goal of a library ought to be the preservation of everybody's right to choose. You do not have to defend everything, although giving in tends to encourage the censors and sets a worrisome precedent. After all, if today you meekly surrender a book or other item to those who want it off the shelves, haven't you seriously weakened your defenses should those same people, emboldened by victory and possessed of the idea that ridding library shelves of "offensive" materials will "clean up the community," come back with a veritable laundry list of other titles that they want to remove?

In general, an individual's attitude towards censorship is the complex result of environment, belief system, and accumulated life experience. Most people acknowledge that they believe reading good books has a positive effect on the human psyche. On the other side is the belief that reading bad or trashy books has a negative effect on the mind and personality of the reader. The operative concern is not whether reading affects attitudes, but whether it affects behavior. If attitudinal shifts are commonly experienced as the result of reading, hearing, or viewing, the only issue becomes whether such attitudinal shifts may be said to cause or produce behavioral shifts. It is all too easy to confuse correlation with causality and the librarian must be extremely careful to avoid mixing one with the other.

All human beings have value systems that define and affect the way in which they lead their lives. Librarians, naturally, also possess value systems and, unless a librarian takes great pains to maintain objectivity (which may never be possible, given human nature), bias will creep into the selection of materials.

Most censorship attempts in libraries arise from the earnest desire of an individual or group to suppress or conceal something from readers, listeners, or viewers, even if that material is true or accurate. But censors do not refer to themselves as censors: he is a watchdog, she is a guardian, he a vigilante, and she a concerned citizen or parent, or simply a worrier about where the world is heading, and how fast. Whether the primary motivation is religious, political, financial, or strictly personal, the effects on the library tend to be the same. The librarian is confronted by a person or group demanding the removal, concealment, labeling, or destruction of materials, with or without stated reasons.

At the outset, the censor's quarrel is not with the librarian, but with the item in question. It isn't until the librarian interposes himself *between* the concerned patron and the material targeted for censorship that interpersonal friction ensues. Such friction usually doesn't lead to legal problems for librarians or their institutions, but the option of recourse to the law is always available. The more alarmed or angry the client becomes, or the more citizens enlisted in the "crusade" against, for example, pornography, the greater the probability that legal action will be taken.

PROMOTION, PUBLICITY, AND PR: MERCHANDISING THE LIBRARY

As with virtually any other service, it is essential for a library's survival to make people aware of its existence and whet their appetite for its services. Larger libraries often hire or designate an existing employee as staff public relations (PR) person or publicist. In most libraries, however, public relations is every staff member's business, as the library attempts to tell its story, portray itself in a desirable light, and maximize the publicity it receives for its achievements.

Along with the obvious and definite need of the library to publicize its services and collections, there is a natural desire to distance itself and its attempts at publicity from that of hard-sell, commercial purveyors of other services. After all, the academic or public library is not a fast-food emporium or an automotive dealership, and techniques of making people aware and interested are, to a great extent, different. Yet there are acknowledged similarities.

Among the library's array of programs, services, and collections, many of potential interest or use merit public awareness. Yet users frequently are ignorant of the opportunities available to them. What is the best way of getting the word out to the community? A first consideration must be funding. If money were no object, there would be no problem in addressing this concern: either buy television and radio airtime, or create a color supplement for the local newspaper, or even direct-mail your desired message to each household in the community. But limited financial resources make most of these options unavailable, unless the various communications media elect to make free time or space available under the rubric of public service programming. Most of the time, the library's budget precludes wholesale broadcast of its message. Clearly, something else must be done, which raises the following issues for information professionals:

- In what ways can the library "advertise" without spending much or any money, yet be certain of getting the library's message to the community?

- What PR techniques can be borrowed from the world of business, for example, which can "market" and "showcase" the library's goods and services and make members of the library's community interested or curious enough to visit the building or call?

- How can favorable word-of-mouth be exploited to a reliable and effective promotion tool?

FUTURING: SCENARIO CONSTRUCTION TECHNIQUES AND METHODOLOGY

Information professionals need to consider where their profession is and where it is going. Perhaps most important, they need to think about where they *want* the profession to go and by what means. This process is sometimes called *futuring*, and it concerns itself both with trends and forecasts and with desirability issues and means to achieve desired ends. The most accessible and non-scientific technique employed by information professionals for projecting some futures for the library is that of the *scenario*, or word-picture. The reason to choose scenario-building, when comparing it to such science-based methods as prediction and projection, is that literally anybody can do it.[6]

Scenarios are used with facility and telling effect to construct possible futures for institutions. They serve as convenient vehicles for laying out alternative approaches to problems of personal or institutional growth and development and then evaluating each, deciding what must happen (or be prevented from happening) to bring it about. Of all techniques used by futurists today, the scenario best permits the investigator to look at problems from different points of view, follow each potential path to its likely denouement, and thereafter have enough insight to choose the preferred paths. Best of all, scenario technique requires no advanced degrees; math, science, or statistical skills; or even computers.

Scenarios are not prophesies or statistics-based projections for institutional outcomes. Conclusive arguments are always hard to come by when one is futuring and facts just don't enter into the discussion. Merely take the institution of concern, apply a generous amount of imagination to the problem, factor in hopes and fears, and come up with alternative scenarios, ranging from depressing ("institutional brain death") to exalted and hopeful ("the nerve center of its community"). The best feature of this technique is simply that a reader who dislikes or disagrees with the selection of another's scenarios is free to write different, more plausible, or better ones. Do not be concerned during this germination phase about the *desirability* of any of your scenarios; that is dealt with later. Futurist Robert Olson asserts that an optimal number of alternative scenarios for a library is three; four at the outside.[7] Such thinking may constitute unnecessary and premature closure of alternatives, however; when brainstorming or "blue-skying" alternative futures, the more there are the better.

Scenarios for a Generic Library

The Death of the Library. To aficionados of libraries, this end may seem chilling, and indeed it is. It's not so much a death in the family, but as though a geriatric family member has moved to Florida, leaving the direction of the family business in younger, less idealistic hands. This scenario offers a "what would happen" look at the library closing its doors for good. It would be a victim of financial impoverishment coupled with the proliferation and wide-spread availability of alternative sources of information and entertainment (e.g., video stores, book rental agencies, 200-channel interactive television cable stations, information brokers), which would pick up any services lost to the community as the result of the demise of the library and possibly provide them more effectively. For that segment of the community with discretionary income for spending on information and recreation, this could prove a boon, with prices kept affordable due to strong competition. As for the other, less affluent component of society, there would be a serious problem, as ability to pay became the prime requirement for library admission or services. A caring government, at the national or state level, might build in some system of "information stamps," whereby the segment of a community below the poverty level would not be excluded from the benefits of such a system, but recent national administrations have shown themselves to be largely indifferent to library matters.

The Library as Robot. This scenario offers a conception of the library applications of interactive robotics. Imagine the library replaced, or, more accurately, merged, with a large and powerful mechanical consciousness, in which patrons in search of documents or facts (or even interpretations) can just contact or come to the library and deal with a humanoid, friendly, and always-available robot who will provide answers in a variety of formats, such as voice, printout, disk, telephone, etc. Considerable work has been done already in the related areas of artificial intelligence and expert systems which make it imaginable that such an amiable android could come clanking (or gliding) over as you enter the library; field your request(s); negotiate and respond to your queries; provide you with reading, viewing, or listening matter; and move smoothly on to the next "patron." It doesn't seem unlikely that such a robot might, in addition to being conversational and helpful, be capable of remembering who you are and what your interests and school assignments were the last time, and further capable of recommending selections, placing orders with publishers, providing security for both personnel and property, opening and closing the building, monitoring internal temperature and air quality, and keeping complete records of all transactions. In fact, the only question here may be that voiced by Marshall McLuhan over twenty-five years ago: displaying a photograph of a small electronic appliance, he asked the unsettling question: "When this printed circuit learns your job, what are you going to do?"[8]

The Status Quo Syndrome. It is possible that the library of twenty-five years hence will be just about the same as that of today because there just won't be enough interest or money to make great changes. Public, academic, and school libraries will neither prosper nor suffer in 2015; they will just plug along pretty much as before, trying to meet the needs of tomorrow's people with what amounts to today's dollars. They will be propelled into the twenty-first century by the pervasive notion in society that libraries are worthy but dull and shouldn't be thrown onto the scrapheap of oblivion, but need no special or dramatic changes in their basic formula. They are therefore permitted to remain, beloved of the few and tolerated by the many, while big, glitzy video stores and private suppliers of materials and services for education, self-improvement, and amusements pass it by.

The Cultural Monument. Related to the scenario just discussed, but even grimmer, is the image of a future library within a society whose citizens agree that "it is fitting and proper that there be a library," but that it should be more of a museum and archive than a lending library or a reference service. On rainy Sunday afternoons, we may take our grandchildren (or *their* kids) into the musty, dusty old library building and, steering them over to a row of glass vacuum cases, point at the relics known as "books," waxing nostalgic about all the books we read (or had to read) when we were young and paper was plentiful. (Note: The next two scenarios collectively known as social engineering, are based on the conviction expressed earlier that the library cannot be *all* things to *all* people and will therefore have to make some tough choices. The most logical, workable choice may be between trying to be *all* things to *some* people and being *some* things to *all* people. Given the present [and projected] status and value [and economic resources] of libraries in public opinion, the library *cannot* be everything to everybody.)

Everything to Some. Under this plan, the library would continue to provide a full run of traditional and new library services to its clientele, but it would be obliged to enact restrictive rules concerning who that clientele might be and/or how they might be assessed for services. Assuming that money remains tight, or grows tighter, the library's entire service philosophy would have to be something like this: richer, more affluent members of the community, who are presumed to have sufficient disposable income to permit them to afford to purchase reading and viewing materials and information, in various formats and amounts, are banned from the library. One's library eligibility is ascertained by requiring users to carry, on an official identification card, a coded infobit (a sort of electronic W-2 record) that classifies one as above, at, or below a variable and floating poverty line. Those below the line receive free library admission and entitlement to all available services without cost. Others may be barred or merely charged proportionately to their ability to pay, on a graduated scale. One benefit of such a system would be its "fairness," meaning that only those wishing to use library services would be obliged to pay for them, while those who prefer to go elsewhere, or do without, would not suffer a financial burden for which they receive no benefits.

In either of these cases, the system would act as a filter: those who can otherwise procure their information/entertainment needs would be obliged to do so or get along as best they can without them, while those in demonstrable need would be entitled to services. In the case of an academic or school library, the student would receive service to the extent of financial need (a form of scholarship award), while the public library would have a graduated scale of prices, depending on the income of the patron. Of course, it would be utopian to suggest or believe that such a system would be universally fair and free from abuses, but what system is perfect?

Some Things for All. This vision of the future library is one in which the institution is obliged to cut back on its previous array of services to its community of users in favor of a leaner line-up of those services. The library would be well advised to select some area of service in which it either excels or is unique. This area could be broad, such as reference and information services, for academic and school libraries, while a public library's scope would be more narrowly focused, as on consumer services, for example, or perhaps community I & R.

Of course, some people would complain at first. Change disrupts almost all of us and threatens more than a few. But if libraries stopped buying and stocking fiction and popular reading, for instance, the move would probably engender the proliferation of bookstores and book rental agencies who would compete for the entertainment or information dollar.

Perhaps the best position for tomorrow's library to be in, assuming that it cannot go on as before, is one in which it markets something not readily and cheaply available in the private sector. Consumer information may be one area which the library can handle well. If a far greater share of the library's budget dollar were put into beefing up free consumer services, it would serve an important social need while ensuring the library's continued claim on public funding far into the next century.

The Experience Parlor. This scenario pertains exclusively to the public library. Imagine that you enter the public library of 2015 to find it totally recast, with the circulation desk transformed into a master control panel and today's reading rooms and stack areas replaced by a series of small cubicles, the size and shape of dentistry treatment rooms, each containing a chair not all that different from present-day dentists' chairs, but with some additional technological equipment. You seat yourself in a large, soft recliner chair, positioned under a helmet-shaped cassette-playing headset which is drawn down over your head, with its electric leads attached to the skull by elastic bands. Now further imagine that a few weeks ago, I joined an expedition to climb Mt. Everest and during the climb wore a headset that recorded my brain waves as I worked my way through the climb: the exhilaration, the ardors, the cold, and the triumph of that expedition. Upon my return the cassette was removed and copied. Now you sit in the chair in the public library/experience parlor, press the "play" button, and the totality of my previously recorded experience is "played" into your head. Even as I went out and climbed that mountain, so do you now, without ever once leaving your chair. As I experienced numbing cold, arduous exercise, emotional highs and lows, oxygen deprivation, etc., so do you now. You don't watch me do it, you are doing it yourself.

No doubt there would be many "bugs" in such a system, some of them quite resistant to solution or removal. Problems concerning this procedure (technical, medical, ethical, moral, legal, financial) would proliferate. Long before such a service became fully operational, vigorous discussion of these matters would be needed in society at large and at various governmental levels. Perhaps even the wisdom and desirability of constructing such systems ought to be debated.

Politicization of the Library. Imagine a future America in which political extremists bring into power a government which, out of a declared security imperative, severely restricts some people's right to enter libraries and drastically curtails the types of materials to be found therein. Under such a regime, academic library access would be the exclusive privilege of those deemed "politically reliable" and, for those lucky enough to gain admission to their public libraries, no information could be found which was at variance or inconsistent with current governmental aims and/or policies. To imagine the rest read George Orwell's *1984*.

In the Privacy of Your Own Home. This title is pretty much self-explanatory, Anyone who has ever experienced the home-shopping channels on cable will grasp this concept at once. Why bother to go to the library if you can send for it? Why borrow (and have to return) material or information, if you already own it? This scenario is not as hi-tech and "blue-sky" as it sounds. Several college and university campuses are "wired" so that students and faculty can access the library's holdings through direct and dial-access hookups.

For public library access, one's home telephone can be used as an input device, while the readout device could be a computer monitor or television screen, a modified FAX, or whatever a twenty-first-century postal system would look like. It might be possible for voice input and output to effect communication with libraries' computers, but that might present too much of a temptation for society to abandon reading. This might happen, anyway, and without catastrophic implications for the quality of life. Still, it is a cherished, time-honored, and first article of today's information professional's faith that reading and books are an unalloyed good. Whether tomorrow's information professionals will share the same view is an interesting if frightening question.

Clearly, this list isn't exhaustive or complete. Perhaps the library will go another way, based on radical technological change. After all, who in 1930 could have imagined the impact of television on us all? If these scenarios for libraries seem displeasing or wrong, write your own better ones.

NOTES

[1] "Librarians Charge Plan Would Cut Flow of Data." *New York Times*, February 21, 1989.

[2] Ellsworth Mason. "Along the Academic Way." *Library Journal* (May 1971): 1675.

[3] Thomas H. Ballard. "More Books, Not Market Surveys." *American Libraries* (February 1981): 76-78.

4 Professor David Kaser, Indiana University, School of Library and Information Science. His celebrated analogy has often been repeated in lectures, classes, and personal conversations over the last two decades, yet never becomes stale.

5 Marshall McLuhan. *The Medium Is the Message: An Inventory of Effects* (New York: Bantam Books, 1967), p. 20.

6 For a discussion of how scenarios are selected, constructed, and evaluated, see Bruce A. Shuman. *The Library of the Future: Alternative Scenarios for Information Professionals* (Englewood, Colo.: Libraries Unlimited, 1989).

7 Robert Olson. "Libraries in the Year 2000." *The Futurist* (November/ December 1988): 51.

8 Marshall McLuhan, 64.

REFERENCE LIST

Information Science

Bellardo, Trudi. "Keeping Up in Information Science." In *Library and Information Science Annual 4*, pp. 3-8. Englewood, Colo.: Libraries Unlimited, 1988.

Diener, Richard A. V. "Information Science: What Is It? ... What Should It Be?" *Bulletin of the American Society for Information Science* 15 (June/ July 1989): 17.

Herner, Saul. "Brief History of Information Science." *Journal of the American Society for Information Science* 35 (May 1984): 157-63.

Schrader, Alvin. "In Search of a Name: Information Science and Its Conceptual Antecedents." *Library and Information Science Research* 6 (July-September 1984): 227-71.

Intellectual Freedom and Censorship

Asheim, Lester. "Not Censorship But Selection." *Wilson Library Bulletin* 28 (September 1953): 63-67.

_____. "Selection and Censorship: A Reappraisal." *Wilson Library Bulletin* 58 (November 1983): 180-84.

Oboler, Eli M. *To Free the Mind: Libraries, Technology, and Intellectual Freedom.* Littleton, Colo.: Libraries Unlimited, 1983.

Office for Intellectual Freedom, American Library Association. *Intellectual Freedom Manual.* 3d ed. Chicago: American Library Association, 1989.

Future of Libraries

Briscoe, Peter, et al. "Ashurbanipal's Enduring Archetype: Thoughts on the Library's Role in the Future." *College and Research Libraries* 46 (March 1986): 121-26.

Gell, Marilyn Mason. "The Future of the Public Library." *Library Journal* 110 (September 1, 1985): 136-39.

Penniman, W. David. "Tomorrow's Library Today." *Special Libraries* 78 (May 1987): 195-205.

Riggs, Donald E., and Gordon A. Sabine. *Libraries in the 90's: What the Leaders Expect.* Phoenix, Ariz.: Oryx Press, 1988.

Shuman, Bruce A. *The Library of the Future: Alternative Scenarios for Information Professionals.* Englewood, Colo.: Libraries Unlimited, Inc., 1989.

Smith, Richard F. "A Funny Thing Is Happening to the Library on Its Way to the Future." *Futurist* 12 (April 1981): 85-91.

Professionalism

Birdsall, William. "Librarianship, Professionalism and Social Change." *Library Journal* 107 (February 1, 1982): 223-26.

Nelson, Bonnie R. "The Chimera of Professionalism." *Library Journal* 105 (October 1, 1980): 2029-33.

Measuring Library Effectiveness

Brown, Willie L. "What Can We Do to Improve the Effectiveness of the Library Lobby?" *U*N*A*B*A*S*H*E*D Librarian* 63 (1987): 18.

Cassell, Kay Ann. *Knowing Your Community and Its Needs.* Chicago: American Library Association, 1988.

Social and Professional Issues

Bender, David. "Transborder Data Flow: An Historical Review and Contributions for the Future." *Special Libraries* 79 (1988): 230-35.

Burgess, Dean. "Fee or Free: The Data Base Access Controversy." *The Reference Librarian* 12 (1985): 105-15.

Childers, Thomas. *The Information Poor in America*. Metuchen, N.J.: Scarecrow Press, 1975.

Cottam, Keith M. "Affirmative Action: Attitude Makes a Difference." *Library Journal* 112 (May 15, 1987): 47-50.

Drake, Miriam A. *User Fees: A Practical Perspective*. Littleton, Colo.: Libraries Unlimited, 1981.

Josey, E. J., ed. *Libraries in the Political Process*. Phoenix, Ariz.: Oryx Press, 1980.

Library Administration and Management Association, American Library Association. *Great Library Promotion Ideas II*, ed. by Ann Heidbreder Eastman and Evelyn Shaeval. Chicago: American Library Association, 1986.

Tarter, Blodwen. "Information Liability: New Interpretations for Electronic Publishing." *Online* (January 1986): 61-67.

U.S. National Commission on Libraries and Information Science. *Task Force on Library and Information Services to Cultural Minorities*. Washington, D.C.: Government Printing Office, 1988.

Wilson, Alex. "The Information Rich and the Information Poor." *ASLIB Proceedings* 39 (January 1987): 1-6.

Wood, Elizabeth J., and Victoria L. Young. *Strategic Marketing for Libraries*. New York: Greenwood Press, 1988. (See especially pages 47-66.)

10 Legal and Ethical Issues Affecting Libraries and Information Centers*

Co-written with Joseph J. Mika

LEGALITIES AND THE LIBRARY

The library, as an institution in the public or private sector, operates under a variety of laws that affect its capabilities and limitations. These laws are not static, but change with the social and political environments at the local, state, and national levels. Librarians of today make more technical decisions in a year than were required of their counterparts of the early 1900s in the entire course of their careers. Technology (e.g., the computer, the laser printer, the modem, teleconferencing) has had a dramatic impact upon the requisite skills and administrative abilities of the librarian. Many librarians, although not specifically identified as administrators, have managerial and decision-making responsibilities. The library, and sometimes the individual librarian, stands a better-than-fair chance of being sued, occasionally for large sums of money, over legal matters not completely understood. It is essential for the information professional to consider the statutory and ethical implications of the laws and rules that directly or indirectly affect library operations and management.

Continual changes in the legal framework and working conditions, and challenges to existing statutes, reflect societal concerns and problems that must be addressed by the librarian, and particularly the library manager, practicing in all types of libraries. This chapter covers matters that are frequently controversial and should stimulate discussion among professionals, administrators, and staff in libraries.

---

*Because of the apparent impossibility of distinguishing ethical from legal concerns in many instances, the two topics are treated together. Some issues are clearly legal, of course, as matters covered by applicable laws. Enough issues are viewed as having both legal *and* moral aspects to justify joint discussion. Issues for discussion are marked with a bullet (•).

PUBLIC LIBRARY LAW

American Library Laws reveals that some state statutes are extremely specific as to what they will (and will not) permit in the way of hiring, firing, and general qualifications of librarians, while other state laws are open to the widest range of interpretation.[1] Illinois state statutes, for example, provide for the hiring of a head librarian by a board of trustees or directors; however, the wording of the statute is more than a little vague. What are the qualifications of a head librarian? As Robert McClarren explains:

> The law is of little help.... The (Illinois) District Library Act only specifies that among the board's powers is that of appointing a "qualified librarian," and the Local Library Act only specifies that the appointment will be a "competent librarian."[2]

What constitutes a "qualified" or "competent" librarian seems to be a matter of individual viewpoint and interpretation. Since the law is hazy on the definition of terms, McClarren provides a few reasonable guidelines, a list of desiderata dealing with the applicant's perceived personal qualities, administrative skills, and professional competencies. Still, "qualified" or "competent" could conceivably be construed as meaning anything from counting and evaluating the degrees possessed by the applicant to merely securing the approval of the mayor or the city manager.

Rarely is the ALA-accredited master of library science degree addressed in library law. Furthermore, only twenty-three states have statutes dealing with certification of librarians. A typical state's (Alabama's) statutory provision for librarians is minimalist, granting the municipal library board the power and authority to:

> 1) Control expenditure of funds appropriated for libraries; 2) Erect or rent buildings; 3) Purchase books and equipment; 4) Provide a system of library service to be made easily available to all citizens of the county or municipality; 5) Elect a librarian and other employees; 6) Manage and control the library; and 7) Keep records of meetings, receipts, and disbursement.[3]

As to the appointment of the head librarian, Arkansas's law states, "The board shall have the power to appoint a librarian qualified by education, training, experience and personality."[4] This certainly provides the board with room for interpretation. The bottom line is that the librarian, almost everywhere, is appointed by the board and serves at its pleasure, subject to termination "for cause." Cause, as one might expect, is left intentionally ambiguous in most states.

Other types of libraries and information centers are governed by their own statutes and laws. For example, academic library law is a function of state laws concerning higher education and school library law frequently entails certification requirements for working in schools.

Study of legislation and its impact on employment is normally assigned to a personnel director or management staff, who update the employer/director at regular intervals. It is often easy to make a mistake in the interview process, to violate an applicant's privacy, or to provide other grounds for lawsuits. For example, statements made in the hiring process have been held to create contractual rights which then preclude at-will termination and set the terms for continued employment.

In the interview, care must be taken to prevent the applicant from assuming that the position is guaranteed "as long as you do a good job, perform satisfactorily, don't screw up, make normal progress, etc." Probationary periods are also being scrutinized, as the successful conclusion of a probationary period may be misinterpreted to mean that the individual has found permanent employment or job security. Instead, the period must be clearly identified in manuals/handbooks as a time of adjustment, the identification of growth needs, matching of employee capabilities with employer needs, and understanding of the responsibilities of the job. For example, school librarians sometimes complain that they are evaluated by their principals and boards according to the same criteria as classroom teachers, rather than as information providers.

EMPLOYEE AND JOB TESTING

Applicants for some library and information center positions are now required to undergo tests mandated by state or local governments. These vary, but among them are (1) medical tests for drug abuse, (2) lie-detector tests to distinguish honest from dishonest employees, (3) written "honesty and reliability" tests to identify potential in-house thieves, (4) personality tests and interviews to screen out various undesirable types of employee behavior, (5) AIDS and other blood screening tests to reveal those with potentially communicable diseases, (6) required medical histories to identify those with predispositions to serious and costly illness, (7) credit checks, and (8) arrest record checks. Federal librarians are frequently subject to testing and employment checks by such agencies as the Federal Bureau of Investigation and the Drug Enforcement Agency.

- What does this screening mean with regard to individual privacy? Does applying for a position in any library or information center require the applicant to submit to a battery of arbitrary, mandated, and invasive tests of suitability? How does an employer's desire to attract and hire the best, most reliable, most productive, and "safest" employees offset the individual's right to privacy, individual freedom, and protection from oppression and surveillance? Lawsuits and court challenges to the use of drug testing are on the rise. In several states, AIDS testing is being challenged as a precondition for employment.

- Do lie detector tests work? Should they be used? Employers, backed by state legislation and the National Labor Relations Act utilize polygraph examinations to verify data on previous employment, medical history, driving record, and criminal convictions.[5] Days Inns of America, a national motel chain, testified in Congress in 1988 that use of lie detectors helped cut its estimated losses from employee crime to $115,000 in 1984, down from $1 million in 1975. Their methodology for arriving at these figures, however, was not revealed. Wrongful discharge suits, in which plaintiffs seek damages for being fired unfairly, routinely appear on the evening news. Are libraries as vulnerable to this threat as for-profit corporations?

• How can libraries, when their employees are accused of causing clients harm, avoid malpractice suits? Malpractice, once only of concern to physicians and attorneys, may become a very real threat to libraries, and is discussed later in this chapter.

• Almost 2 million lie detector (polygraph) tests are given to employees and job applicants in the United States each year. A labor lawyer describes them as being a "very effective tool in stopping employee crime," but are they more a deterrent to crime or an effective means of determining an employee's guilt or innocence?

• Some of the psychological tests were discussed in a *Newsweek* cover story in 1986. How would you like your answers or your expressed level of agreement with these statements to determine *your* suitability for the job you presently hold?

   1) "People are honest because they are afraid of being caught"; 2) "I worry about sexual matters"; 3) "I feel unhappy most of the time"; 4) "Sometimes there is a feeling like something is pressing on my head"; 5) "There are those out there who want to get me"; 6) "The things that run through my head sometimes are horrible"; 7) "I have headaches more and more frequently"; 8) "I am often very tense on the job"; and 9) "I wish I could do over some of the things I have done."[6]

Some corporations whose employees will routinely be handling large sums of money are subjected to an "honesty test" that includes such questions as:

1. If you saw another person stealing on the job, would you turn that person in to the boss?

2. Did you ever cheat in school?

3. Do you believe everyone is dishonest to a certain degree?

4. When you are wrong, do you usually admit it?

5. Do you ever worry about what other people think of you?

6. Have you ever made a mistake on any of your jobs?

These questions are fraught with peril, because giving answers which are "too correct" or "too pure" may brand the respondent as a potential liar, or worse. A new Massachusetts state law prohibits employers from giving honesty tests that amount to "paper and pencil" polygraphs.

The U.S. Chamber of Commerce estimates that drug (and alcohol) abuse among workers costs employers $60 billion a year in lost productivity, accidents, higher medical claims, absenteeism, and theft of company property to finance workers' drug habits.

- The Reagan administration proposed, some years ago, that the U.S. government adopt pre-hire drug testing.[7] What effect would this have on federal librarians and those working as federal contractors?

- Then there are drug tests. Are such tests constitutional, fair, or even accurate detectors of dishonesty or maladjustment? "Many legal scholars believe that there ... exists in society a certain essential right of individuals to be left alone, and not to be subjected to ... invasive activities without justification."[8]

EMPLOYEE TESTS AND LIBRARY STAFF

The information profession is somewhat different from banking or stock brokering. Librarians do not routinely handle large sums of money. The contents of the petty cash drawer and the month's fine money normally do not motivate employees to commit larceny. Yet there are enough cases on record involving pilferage of library funds, equipment, and supplies to justify concern.

- Is there an ethical difference between stealing $30 in fine money and stealing $30,000 through embezzlement or computer crime? The only difference is one of degree. Public libraries are increasingly being told by city governments that they must administer tests to new and/or incumbent employees; generally they cannot refuse to comply.

- Library staff members and potential staff members are sometimes subjected to scrutiny of their private lives, which constitutes a different type of test. Probing into personal lives may be viewed either as an unreasonable invasion of privacy or a prudent means of identifying problem employees before they create or become problems.

  Extremely subjective measures of employee suitability are not only utilized, but supported by legal and judicial bodies. In one case, the Supreme Court of the United States let stand a lower court decision permitting a public library in Pennsylvania to dictate the sexual conduct and family living arrangements of its employees.[9] At issue was more than just the lifestyles of library employees; this case involved a challenge to the equal protection clause of the Fourteenth

Amendment to the Constitution. In this case, the library board attempted to dissuade a pair of library colleagues from living together. They refused, and both were fired.

• Does lifestyle pertain to one's job performance?

AFFIRMATIVE ACTION AND DISCRIMINATION PROBLEMS

"Accept the premise that Affirmative Action is the law of the land and compliance is in the best interest of all of us. It's going to happen," states Keith Cottam.[10] Women and minorities have been the principal beneficiaries of affirmative action legislation. Few claim that the law is universally fair, or that no one is injured as a result of its provisions, but libraries, like other types of institutions, must comply with the law.

Is it possible to discriminate in favor of one group of people, for any reason at all, without discriminating against other groups? Is this justifiable? The Supreme Court has ruled that the race and/or sex of an individual can be used as one of several factors to be weighed in the hiring and promotion of employees. This may lead to job preferences for women and minority group members in jobs or occupations traditionally and historically dominated by white males. Other decisions have upheld the use of numerical quotas for promoting members of minority groups in specific industries or job classifications. Ironically, discrimination has become necessary to remedy the inequities caused by discrimination.

Federal government legislation affecting libraries and other information agencies, such as the Equal Employment Opportunity Act, is not universally applauded. Cottam states that: "Some librarians think they now have more to worry about ... in hiring, disciplining, promoting and compensating employees."[11] Others lament unwanted governmental interference in what used to be private, or at least local, practice and procedure.

Actually, affirmative action is only one of the legal ramifications of equal employment opportunity, a convenient phrase which bears significantly upon such issues as employee selection, pay equity, seniority, age discrimination, the hiring of the handicapped, sexual harassment, pregnancy and maternity leave, pensions, religious freedom, veterans' preferences, and the rights of AIDS victims.[12]

The American Library Association has reflected both societal and professional concerns about fairness in employment and, subsequent to the passage of pertinent laws, it has issued policy statements concerning equal employment opportunity, pay equity, and related matters. Affirmative action and other laws and rules are controversial, but they are generally felt to be both necessary and desirable to correct previous inequities. Even though some blameless individuals may be discriminated against in the process, positive long-range effects are expected.

In the fight for sexual equality in public library employment, other actions are being taken. In June 1987, *American Libraries* reported that a group called Ohio Women Librarians (OWL) stated that 80 percent of the state's largest public libraries were directed by males in 1985.[13]

- Is this cause for alarm or remedial action? Can this situation be corrected or adjusted without laws that work against some while promoting the interests of others? *Should* this situation be corrected? "Through collective action, group pressure, scrutiny by citizens and public officials, advocacy, support, and education efforts, the oppressed female majority in Ohio libraries can achieve equity."[14]

- What else can be done in and for libraries and information centers before legislative action is required?

SEXUAL HARASSMENT

When does sexual interest become sexual harassment? This is a difficult form of behavior to define: one person's off-color remark may well be another's witticism, ineptitude, or innocence. Jo Cates, in an article in *Library Journal*, cites inappropriate (and possibly even illegal) questions asked of female applicants at a job interview, the most outrageous being: "How much of your salary will you spend on birth control devices?"[15]

The *American Heritage Dictionary* defines "harass" as "to irritate or torment persistently." Sexual harassment charges are filed under Title VII of the Civil Rights Act of 1964. Three items must be present in sexual harassment cases: (1) the harassment must be of a sexual nature; (2) it must be a condition of employment; and (3) the harassing employee must be in a supervisory capacity. In 1980, the Equal Employment Opportunity Commission provided a regulation on sexual harassment, defining it as a form of sex discrimination. In one interesting case, other forms of unwelcomed behavior, not explicitly sexual, may still be sexual harassment if they would not have occurred but for a victim's sex.

Michigan's Task Force on Sexual Harassment in the Workplace decreed that sexual harassment, in addition to fondling or groping without consent, included any or all of the following: continual or repeated verbal abuse of a sexual nature including, but not limited to, graphic commentaries on the victim's body; sexually suggestive objects or pictures in the workplace; sexually degrading words used to describe the victim, or propositions of a sexual nature, and the threat or insinuation that lack of sexual submission will adversely affect the victim's employment, wages, advancement, assigned duties or shifts, academic standing, or other conditions that affect the victim's livelihood.[16]

The U.S. Merit Systems Protections Board report on sexual harassment in the federal workplace frames its definition of the term by listing the following as constituting sexual harassment: (1) actual or attempted rape or sexual assault; (2) uninvited pressure for sexual favors; (3) uninvited and deliberate touching; (4) leaning over, cornering, or pinching; (5) uninvited sexually suggestive looks or gestures; (6) uninvited pressures for dates; and (7) uninvited sexual teasing, jokes, remarks, or questions.[17]

Frequently the decision of guilt or innocence of harassment comes down to one person's word against another's. The question is often, when is it sexual harassment and when is it only harmless office flirtation? One person's appreciative glance might be another person's suggestive look, and still another's leer. Who is to decide, and on what criteria, and what should the penalties for the guilty be? In every case, the operative word is *uninvited* (or maybe unwanted), but even this is open to interpretation.

CRIME IN LIBRARIES

Alan Lincoln, a professor of law, defines crime in legalistic terms, noting that the perception of crime may be subjective, but the legal definition of crime is specific. That is, there may be a difference between what an observer calls a crime and what really, according to law, *is* a crime. "Crime is an intentional act or omission in violation of criminal law..., committed without defense or justification, and sanctioned by the state as a felony or misdemeanor."[18]

State or local statute determines what defines a crime for a legal jurisdiction. Lincoln adds: "In contrast to law is social deviance. Many actions that are considered unacceptable by the general public are not illegal but deviant. Most behavior falls within the limits of what is considered normative or acceptable."[19]

Whether actions are considered acceptable also depends on the setting. Behavior that is considered appropriate in one's own home may be perceived as deviant if demonstrated in the school or library. Since deviance is a social concept with individual differences in definition, it is not surprising that people disagree on the range of appropriate behavior. Much disruptive but non-criminal behavior that affects libraries may be a problem of different standards being used by different people.

Some clearly illegal actions are tolerated, if not exactly condoned and are largely excused as too minor to warrant action. Consequently, library patrons and law enforcement agencies often fail to take such problems seriously. Book theft, for example, is not always regarded as sufficiently serious to initiate prosecution, which is difficult, expensive, time-consuming, problematical from a public relations standpoint, and frequently yields little return for the effort. The problem often rests with the library staff. If they do not consider such behavior as crime, they cannot hope to persuade others of the very real cost of such activity and the need for legal action.

Crime in libraries includes book, material, and equipment theft; vandalism; mutilation; arson; disruptive patron behavior; assault (against patrons or staff); drug trafficking (presumably by patrons, not librarians); and variant types of behavior always a problem for public buildings, such as exhibitionism, indecent exposure, and voyeurism.

In academic and school libraries and media centers, the use and sale of drugs in the library constitutes a crime, while misdemeanor charges may be brought against students who smoke, drink alcoholic beverages, or otherwise misbehave. The true definition of library crime, like obscenity, is in the eye of the beholder. And, like obscenity, it is prosecuted according to the applicable state or local law or ordinance.

Crime, however, is committed not only by patrons but by employees. Embezzlement, fraudulent appropriation of property, book theft, inappropriate use of time, and wrongful use of supplies and equipment are just a few of the illegal activities. Employees of American businesses were stealing an estimated $8.5 to 9 billion a year in goods and services from their employers two decades ago.[20] One writer states: "It is as important for the administration to consider crime perpetrated by employees as it is by patrons."[21]

- Have we sufficient reason to believe that libraries are different from businesses in this respect?

- In our schools, teachers sometimes request information of librarians, stating that they need to know which students have checked certain books or other media out, especially when they are overdue. Perhaps more frightening is the case of the parent who says: "I have a right to know what books and videos my child checks out of this library, since I am going to be financially liable if they aren't returned." Do they have valid points?

Summing up, libraries are forced to deal with a bewildering array of complex, contradictory, and discriminatory laws which they must work with and within, affecting virtually every area of the workplace. While it may be frustrating and difficult, we must work with existing laws until better, clearer statutes came along.

Since legal matters are complex and intricate, what can or should librarians and library administrators do to protect themselves against expensive mistakes?

THE FREEDOM OF INFORMATION ACT, PRIVACY, AND CONFIDENTIALITY

- What would be your reaction to law enforcement officers requesting access to the borrowing records of individuals or requiring the compilation of a list of persons borrowing materials on explosives? Imagine your feelings and reactions when informed by the FBI that providing this information will safeguard democracy. If you refuse, are you being unpatriotic? If you comply, are you betraying the public trust?[22]

- Is cooperation with law enforcement agents to be viewed as the violation of an implicit relationship between the librarian and the patron, much like that between clergy and congregation, lawyers and clients, and physicians and patients?[23]

- Is refusal to divulge information about patrons' borrowing habits and records to law enforcement authorities consistent with the principle of privacy and confidentiality of patron records? Suppose refusal might lead to legal and ethical problems for both the librarian and the library, including subpoenas of records, obstruction of justice charges, and accessory to, or complicity in, criminal actions. What then?

Ethical concerns about duty, obligation to society, and being true to oneself are involved in this scenario. It is wise to think through the consequences of compliance and of non-compliance with such requests. Public trust is at stake, as is a matter of conscience.

• Are public records, by definition, public and viewable on demand?

• Does one set of rules apply to minors and another to persons no longer minors? This point is open to interpretation and frequently to litigation[24]

• Will such problems resolve themselves as libraries automate their records and install circulation systems that encumber records in charging out materials, deleting records automatically upon return?

PROBLEM PATRONS IN LIBRARIES

Library literature (especially that concerned primarily with public libraries) abounds with articles on problem patrons and the library's *legal* powers and limitations (ethical concerns are dealt with later in this chapter) in dealing with them. In Ann Arbor, Michigan, a library rule permitting staff to banish or to remove from the building patrons with offensive odors was successfully challenged and overturned. The director then challenged *that* ruling, regaining the power to turn away those whose persons interfered with others' ability to enjoy the library in comfort.[25] The pivotal issue is whether the library policy was judged to violate the right of persons to enter and use the building freely.

• Is lack of personal hygiene sufficient legal cause for removal from a public building? Most "nuisance" conditions or behavior, while annoying both to staff and patrons, are not sufficient grounds for legal action.

• Should libraries establish and display lists of unacceptable patron behaviors? These may vary, based upon circumstances. What is considered eccentric and relatively harmless in one person may be deemed threatening and frightening in another. Consider: You are a female librarian, seated at your desk in a public area of the library. A woman appearing to be in her late sixties or early seventies, short of stature and gentle of manner, stares fixedly at you throughout your entire two-hour shift. What do you do? Maybe you remind her of her daughter, married and living elsewhere. Most librarians would probably smile, even approach the woman offering assistance, making small talk, etc. Now imagine the same situation, only this time the patron staring at you is a burly male, dressed in work clothes, and over six feet tall. Would you smile at him, ask him questions, make polite conversation? Probably not. Yet the nature of the situation is exactly the same in the eyes of most applicable state and local statutes: staring at someone without making insinuating remarks or threatening gestures is not sexual harassment or considered worthy of either summoning the police or asking the patron to cease and desist his behavior or leave the building.

- What should be done about patron behavior that cannot be construed as criminal, yet which many people find annoying, if not frightening? In a curious sense, criminal behavior in the library may well be the easiest to deal with, because it is the easiest to define.

- If feeling threatened, but not witnessing overt menacing behavior, should the librarian summon help by calling security or the police, and apologize later if need be? Why or why not?

- What action should a public, academic, or school librarian take when teenagers, necking in public, annoy other patrons? Certainly this is inappropriate behavior in the library, but under what statute or written rule can you justify expulsion, and would the punishment fit the crime?

- Suppose a patron mutters constantly under his breath and will not (or cannot) stop, even when asked? If repeated requests and warnings are ignored, have you the right to demand that he leave?

- What is appropriate when persons bring food into the library and use worktables for picnics? By the time you reach them they're usually finished, and reading or pretending to read.

- When persons sleep in the library, or only come to use the restrooms and warm themselves, is that inappropriate use of facilities?

    Remember that demanding that people leave when they are only sitting innocently at a table can create a public relations problem when your actions are witnessed by others.

- What if exhibitionists and voyeurs (flashers and peepers) are reported? Indecent exposure may possibly be classed as assault, depending on exactly what is done, and to whom, but it is frequently difficult to catch flashers. Peepers are even harder to apprehend and fervent denials are difficult to disprove.

- In all types of libraries, people carry on loud conversations, ignoring others who expect that a relative degree of quiet will be maintained. How do you get them to observe common courtesy?

- When people smoke in non-smoking areas and a lecture will not produce a change in behavior, is throwing them out the correct response?

- What would you do when street people, who seem to live out of one or two shopping bags and have no other place to be and who frequently smell bad, take up residence in the library? Even when such people make it impossible, or at least difficult, to breathe or function in their vicinity, judges and coalitions have interfered with the right of librarians to eject them. Besides, on a cold or rainy day, how do you feel about tossing such unfortunates out into the elements?

- If people ask annoying or inappropriate questions or ask the same questions repeatedly, what action should be taken? Some are lonely, some retarded, a few embittered, distracted, deranged, or malevolent.

- When dealing with problem patrons, how can librarians "know when to hold 'em and know when to fold 'em?" Can training or experience best help us to acquire an understanding of which problems can be handled personally and which require the assistance or enforcement of others or of the law?

HIRING, FIRING, EVALUATION, AND COLLECTIVE BARGAINING

With regard to their protection against legal claims, most information professionals have yet to experience the types of malpractice suits prevalent in the legal and medical professions, but librarians as administrators have been subjected to legal action involving the interviewing, hiring, salary increases, promotion, evaluation, and firing of employees.[26] In many instances, labor unions representing municipal school or academic employees have a great deal of impact on hiring, promotion, and termination. Mary Hutchings Reed gives a lucid account of litigation that has involved librarians and libraries, brought under federal statutes, including the Civil Rights Act (1964) (Title VII), the Equal Pay Act (1963), the Rehabilitation Act (1973), the Age Discrimination Act (1975), and the Age Discrimination in Employment Act, and under the First, Fifth, and Fourteenth Amendments to the United States Constitution.[27]

Collective Bargaining

- Is interest in unionization an abandonment of professional status, or is it a means to achieving status? Unions sometimes provide the broad political base necessary for the negotiation of librarians' concerns. However, collective bargaining does not guarantee an improvement in the role of librarians in institutional governance—that role is still to be won at the bargaining table. Management does not lose the right to manage because a collective bargaining agent is elected. While influence on policy increases with unionization, the influence generally does not extend beyond subjects that traditionally involve librarian participation. All too often, collegiality is replaced by a labor-management environment.[28]

Collective bargaining between library employees and management has developed, within the last twenty years, into a major concern for the library personnel administrator. Although the first library union was formed in 1914, unionization has become a significant factor only within the past two decades. This increased interest is rooted in the passing of federal and state legislation that allows private and public sector unionization.

The system governing labor relations for librarians is based upon the industrial model of labor-management relations, as outlined in the National Labor Relations Act and amended by the Labor Management Relations Act, in which the union and employer are distinct legal entities with rights and obligations established by law. The past six decades of unionization and collective bargaining have involved a series of governmental actions that have resulted in see-saw policies and actions that appear to favor the employer and the employee in alternating cycles.

Impetus for unionization varies from institution to institution, but generally includes one or more of the following: dissatisfaction with management decisions; discontent with increasing administrative dominance; concern over the economic condition of the institution/library and increasing external control; discontent over low salaries, minor salary increases, and unsatisfactory working conditions; desire for increased role in governance; lack of job security; and concern over the retrenchment (or possible retrenchment) of colleagues.

- Is collective bargaining a remedy or cure for these problems in libraries and information centers?

  Unfortunately, the relationship that is then established is generally adversarial. Often lost in creating this relationship is the realization that the individuals involved are the same as those prior to the establishment of collective bargaining, seeking a humane, shared approach to negotiations and resulting governance under contract as a goal.

- In what ways can library employees use the strength that the union vehicle provides, but temper this strength with professionalism? And how can administrators view collective bargaining as a tool that allows, defines, and limits the employees' position and role in institutional decision making?

Generally, the status of most unionized librarians remains virtually the same as before collective bargaining. In only four areas may advancements in librarians' situations be seen: salary improvement, evaluation, promotion, and tenure. If librarians have not gained much by their involvement in collective bargaining, it may be because we have generally stayed away from becoming too involved politically in the higher levels of our institutions.

- Is greater involvement in the political arenas of our institutions so that we may have an impact upon information policy (which will also affect our working environments) overdue?

Collective bargaining is but one way to achieve our goals. It has produced mixed results to date, but it is a vehicle that may be utilized effectively. More important, librarians must study employers and administrators to find out what attracts their attention and what produces favorable results.

- If we seek to establish ourselves in the political and informational mainstream of the institution and if the top administrator is the chief executive officer (CEO), then how can we begin to have him perceive our positions as those of CIOs, "chief information officers?"

  Since no one in the parent organization is better prepared to do what we do—acquire, organize, find, and provide important information—what steps can we take to make administrators fully realize and appreciate our worth and contributions?

COPYRIGHT LAW AND LIBRARIES

Copyright is a legal term that has been around for over a century. It refers to the legal right of a person who claims proprietary intellectual property to have, among other rights, the exclusive right to sell copies of an original work and to sell new works that are based upon or derived from that original work. In recent years, numerous significant developments pertaining to copyright as it affects librarians and libraries have occurred while previous issues have intensified in importance.[29]

Until fairly recently copyright in libraries was not a significant problem for librarians and educators because wholesale copying of documents was slow, cumbersome, and expensive and produced, for the most part, unsatisfactory results. Recent technological developments and the proliferation of automation and photocopying equipment have made copying simple, convenient, and difficult to detect, which places members of the library profession at risk of charges of infringement of copyright, whether intentional or unintentional.

In recent years, numerous significant developments affecting copyright issues and principles in the United States have taken place in the courts, in Congress, and especially in the U.S. Copyright Office, a division of the Library of Congress. There are many players in these events—publishers, authors, artists, wholesalers, teachers, librarians, attorneys—and just about anybody who copies more than a page or two is affected, in some way, by the provisions of the Copyright Law.

Curiously, the actual stated purpose of federal copyright law, which is continually under revision (the last formal revision was in 1988), is not so much to protect the financial interests of publishers as it is "to promote the creation and dissemination of knowledge and ideas." In other words, copyright may serve to protect producers of information from diminution of their revenues, but its ostensible purpose is that of inducing sharing of that information, for the mutual benefit of all.

First, let us consider the magnitude of the problem. Whereas most commodities (such as lumber, beef, or pencil sharpeners) are subject to certain laws of supply and demand, meaning that one cannot have something and give it away or sell it, also, information is copiable. The ease and ready availability of copying technology, together with the flaws of human nature result in all sorts of unlawful copying every day.

In monetary terms, estimates vary as to how much these practices are costing publishers and authors. A higher estimate is that between $43 billion and $61 billion annually is lost to those legally entitled to it because of infringement and piracy, without taking into consideration thousands of jobs lost each year because of closed or curtailed publishing interests. These sums are staggering and may be exaggerated to drive home a point, but the negative effects of such losses are quite real.

The only legal way to copy material under copyright protection is by express written permission of the copyright holder. Yet extensive abuse of this simple rule occurs all the time. Clearly, there are many and far-reaching ethical and legal ramifications of copying, and the putative victims, authors and publishers, want something done. After all, the creation of an intellectual property is difficult, laborious, time consuming, and frequently expensive for author and publisher. A reasonable return on one's investment is expected. Anything that diminishes that return constitutes a threat to one's inclination and ability to continue writing or publishing materials.

The U.S. Copyright Law is intended to provide and preserve incentive to creativity by protection of the financial interests of those whose livelihoods are dependent upon production of such works and to prohibit (and punish) misuse of copyrighted materials.

So it is that current copyright law involves itself with a concept called *fair use*, by which is meant the extent of copying or other reproduction of copyrighted materials, *without permission*, that is considered both legally and ethically "fair." This is a difficult concept, open to a variety of interpretations and assailable on many grounds.

Fair use has to do with such matters as the purpose of the copying, the nature of the work copied, the amount or portion of the total work to be copied, and, perhaps most important, the effect of the use, in the sense of who will profit from the copying. There are various tests that one is expected to apply to see whether the proposed use constitutes fair use. These tests may be paraphrased as a series of questions to be posed prior to copying the work. For example, can the copy be substituted for the purchase? For what reason is the work to be copied? What is the benefit of the copying to society or to a specific institution? Did the impulse to copy come spontaneously, leaving the would-be copier no time to secure permission? Is the portion of the work to be copied sufficiently small (e.g., the law permits copying fewer than 250 words of a poem and no more)? Will the copied document display a valid warning of criminal prosecution in a prominent place? Is only *one* copy of the work to be made?

Copyright is an area of problems for libraries that extends to, and beyond, such topics as interlibrary loan, reserves, audio and visual materials, classroom use, software, off-air taping, instructional modules, and the campus-wide policies of academic institutions. Space limitations preclude a protracted discussion of these matters, but every librarian should have read, and be conversant with, the current provisions of copyright law.

- What shall we do about the pervasive notion that the Copyright Law is unenforceable and that transgressors won't get caught?

- Is copyright infringement a relatively minor offense, because everybody's doing it?

Every now and again, an angry or distraught publisher decides to try to make an example of someone caught infringing its copyright and directs its corporate lawyers to prosecute that party to the fullest extent of the law. Penalties may range from fines to imprisonment and, when found guilty, the malefactor is given the widest possible media coverage. This provides a "chilling effect," as it is supposed to do, which may discourage others tempted to break the law from so doing. But litigation is very expensive and time consuming and seldom results in profitable adjustments. Besides, there is the problem that the librarian, acting only as a facilitator for copying, might inadvertently aid or abet a crime, through permitting the institutional facilities and equipment to be used in unauthorized copying of protected material.

- Since copyright law is, and will no doubt continue to be, a confusing welter of unenforceable provisions and vague conditions, what are some ways for a library to protect itself against the commission of crimes and the risk of ruinous lawsuits?

- Can the information professional, by examining his own conscience, work out an internal code of behavior that is both consistent with existing law and satisfying, as much as possible, to all participants? This mention of conscience will serve as an appropriate segue into the related area of ethics, which is closely intertwined with the legal matters discussed thus far.

ETHICS AND THE LIBRARIAN

Before dealing with ethics in detail, it seems appropriate to begin with some discussion of *The Librarian's Code of Ethics* (see Appendix A), a document of high, lofty professional principle. Our profession's ethical code, however, may appear to connote an attitude tantamount to a monk's vows of poverty. While a monk places dedication to public service above personal or financial gain; however, our ethical code should not be interpreted to imply that information professionals do not have the right and responsibility to fight for improved salaries. Seeking augmented compensation is not incompatible with professional conduct and our service ethic does not necessarily prevent us from doing what many other professional groups do to demonstrate their worth to society. As a group we are simply too modest and altruistic to proclaim our legitimate need for better salaries. This does not necessarily mean that strikes and other job actions are forbidden to professional librarians, unless they are illegal for all employees of the institution. But it is demonstrable that comparatively few librarians withhold their services (through strikes and other job actions) in attempts to compel their employers to augment salaries. Conventional wisdom views libraries as unexciting places, inessential to one's quality of life. So it is with the popular perceptions of librarians: demure and unassuming and not in need of high salaries.

The area of ethics is one in which, unlike the law, no clear-cut distinctions are possible. While the study of ethics deals with right and wrong, and telling one from another, there are actually no absolute "rights" and "wrongs" in ethics; there are, rather, interpersonal differences, as each person marches to the beat of a different drummer and answers to his own conscience.

Definitions

Ethics is commonly considered to be the study of moral action, motives, or character. This includes what is professionally right or fitting. In everyday parlance, we think of ethics in terms of "right" and "wrong" and leave morality to the clergy to define. Ethics may be understood to be the rules and accepted values that identify or indicate what is acceptable as right and good, or which conform to professional standards of conduct. Collectively, they are an extension and a summation of a society's culture and, as such, they tend to change as community values change.

Unlike morality, which many see as God-defined and religious in origin and practice, ethics are personal, involving not so much what is permitted and prohibited or what is legal or illegal, but that which evokes matters of individual conscience. It is difficult, perhaps impossible, to codify or to achieve consensual agreement about ethics. While most people strive to practice ethical behavior, the issues involved in ethical decisions are never simple or clear-cut.[30]

Ethics has emerged as one of the "hottest" and most dominant topics in recent times. It transcends disciplines. The resignation of several members of the United States Congress and of other high-level government officials has brought the political ramifications of ethical matters into sharp focus. In some institutions of higher education, centers for ethics and ethical issues are being organized and given program status, while at the same time, the occupational title "ethicist" is being added to the ranks of professional workers. Many of these centers and institutes are the product of interdisciplinary cooperation, with hybrid courses created bearing such titles as "The Ethics of Management," "The Ethics of Medical Practice," "The Ethics of Biology," "Ethics for Librarianship," and "The Philosophy of Ethical Behavior."

Health institutions are hiring professional ethicists who counsel practitioners on the ethics of life-and-death decisions, such as when to take patients off life-support systems and when life may be said to begin or end. While programs of library education usually include a lecture, or even a few sessions, on the ethics of librarianship in an introductory course, it is only in recent years that library schools, following national trends, are giving more than cursory attention to the topic. An Allerton Park conference sponsored by The School of Library and Information Science of the University of Illinois, held in October 1989, identified as its theme "Ethics and the Librarian." It is probably safe to assume that all ALA-accredited library schools are now discussing ethical issues in their curricula and debating whether to add ethics components to each course or to create a separate course on the topic.

Interest in ethics has recently been reborn because of the implications of new technology and our ability to apply developing knowledge to our lives. For example, the ability to transplant body parts from cadavers to the living raises psychological and social questions and emotions that bring ethics into play.

We frequently read about the issue (now highlighted by the interest of the last two presidents) of abortion, which involves the rights of a mother versus the rights of her fetus. Add to this issue, which has both legal and ethical aspects, such controversial matters as euthanasia, the right to die, genetic reproduction, and genetic engineering, and it is readily apparent why ethics are now of major interest.

The Librarian's Code of Ethics

Librarians' professional activities (ethics for information science are elaborated in a separate document, discussed later in this chapter) are governed by a code of ethics (1982), promulgated by the ALA (see appendix A). The code is historically rooted in principles suggested to guide the actions of librarians as far back as the 1930s. The ALA notes 1939 as the formal beginning of recognition of professional ethics. Interest in ethics grew and broadened over the following three decades, culminating in the formulation of the code during the 1970s, a period of strong interest in personal and professional ethics and social activity.

Ethics, Confidentiality, and Privacy of Library Records

In addition to the legal implications of confidentiality laws, there are also numerous ethical facets of the confidentiality issue. The ALA's Statement on Professional Ethics (1981) includes the following: "Librarians must protect each user's right to privacy with respect to information sought or received, and materials consulted, borrowed, or acquired."[31] This seems, at first blush, an unarguable statement, a simple affirmation that our professional charge, responsibility, and duty is to ensure that library patrons need not fear that outside persons might, through investigation of their reading habits, draw conclusions regarding their previous, present, or future behavior. In this manner, the professional relationship of librarian and client bears a resemblance to the relationship of priest to parishoner, physician to patient, and attorney to client. In those cases, however, the law joins with codes of ethics to protect the practitioner from divulging the content of conversations or discussions. For libraries, however, the code of ethics alone stands between our professional practice and the requirement to disclose or turn over the sometimes sensitive nature of our borrower's reading, viewing, or listening tastes.

Consider the case of John Hinckley, Jr., who, in May 1981, determined that the quickest, best way to impress actress Jodie Foster favorably would be to assassinate the president of the United States. Upon learning of Hinckley's deed, reporters and law enforcement authorities assailed Hinckley's Colorado hometown public library, seeking to learn his borrowing habits, his taste in literature, whether he returned his materials on time, and whatever else might help explain (and sensationalize) his attempt on the life of the president. Citing various federal and state legislation dealing with open records, police in various parts of the nation sought to gain access to the borrowing behavior of other suspected criminals, members of clandestine organizations, and just plain "weirdos." The issue centered on whether public library records, whether computerized, microform, printed, or handwritten, could be considered public documents and therefore available for inspection by virtually anyone upon demand.

Ours is a nation of laws, and subpoenas demanding the production of specified documents, signed by legally empowered judges, must be obeyed. Failure to comply may very easily lead to fine or imprisonment. Consider what you might do when confronted with one of these possible situations:

- While working as an information professional, you accidentally find, concealed in a library book, a note threatening death to a public official. Do you inform the local police of your discovery? Upon request by the police, would you furnish the name of the last borrower of the book?

- The police have learned that a crude, homemade incendiary device has been used to blow up and burn a local clinic where abortions are performed. The next day, two detectives visit your library and request the names of all persons who have checked out books on bombs, explosives, weapons, guerrilla warfare, and revolutionary strategies in the past six months.

- You are speaking to the civic Rotary organization on the topic of interesting new books and you happen to note in passing, to show your devotion to intellectual freedom, that the library has recently purchased the latest controversial sex manual and that some of the town's leading citizens have already placed their names on the reserve list for it. After your talk, a library board member wants to look at the names of those leading citizens waiting to read the book, citing idle curiosity, but pointing out that such records are not private but public.

- Some "concerned parents" want to know whether their daughter has been borrowing books on witchcraft or the occult from the public library.

- The same parents want to know the names of *all* high-school-aged (or younger) persons who have been investigating the subject of witchcraft.

- You, as an academic library reference librarian, are asked by members of the Federal Bureau of Investigation to report requests for materials in science or engineering by persons who have accents that seem "Slavic" or from persons who have "Russian-sounding" names.

- Quite recently, a Queens, New York, grand jury ordered the New York Public Library to release loan records to detectives who are trying to apprehend a gunman popularly known as the Zodiac killer, believed responsible for shooting four people in six months. Investigators suspect that he may be inspired by a certain 1904 book, which he may have borrowed from the library. The library complied with the subpoena, stating that it was reluctant to do so, but to refuse would have been unlawful.

A word of warning: it is relatively simple to proclaim that you would fearlessly uphold the right to privacy of each patron, a position so strongly endorsed in our professional literature. But just suppose that you thought that, by "bending just a bit," you might prevent a capital crime or an explosion causing considerable loss of property and life.

The point of this discussion of right of confidentiality and privacy for our patrons is that there is no clear line between what is right and what is wrong in deciding which records will be kept under lock and key to protect our patrons from unwarranted invasion of privacy and which records are and should be available for inspection by the police, the library's board members, the clergy, or other patrons.[32] The ALA's code of ethics states clearly that "Librarians must protect each user's right to privacy with respect to information sought or received and materials consulted, borrowed, or acquired." But circumstances, and your own considered feelings, will no doubt dictate whether you, when placed on the spot, adhere strictly to that statement or find some other way through this sometimes featureless ethical terrain.

Librarians versus the FBI

Imagine that two or more large, intimidating men, representing the federal, state, or local government, sit you down in a small room and inform you that your cooperation is a duty, may save lives, will be held in the strictest confidence, and will save you from certain unspecified but implied adverse consequences. What do you do then? And a further disturbing thought: what if you "do the right thing" and refuse to cooperate with law enforcement authorities in their fishing expeditions, and then, that night, on the 11 o'clock news, you learn that some horrible and heinous deed was committed and the perpetrators are believed to have acquired the knowledge and abilities to do what they have done through books. *Library* books! Can you be certain that you will be able to sleep the sleep of the just and the innocent, merely because you didn't kill anyone directly? Are you, technically, at least, an accessory to the crime because you could have tried to prevent it, yet didn't? From this and other examples in this chapter, it is not difficult to see how ethical challenges can easily become legal problems, with penalties that go far beyond the qualms of conscience.

In case you think this scenario is farfetched, consider that when the remaining members of the Symbionese Liberation Army were arrested in San Francisco, a search of the apartment of two of the group's members disclosed several books on counter-insurgency and guerilla warfare, checked out from various area libraries and never returned.

In recent years, both commercial and professional literature and the broadcast airwaves have been filled with accounts of the Federal Bureau of Investigation's (FBI's) Library Awareness Program, together with much emotional debate over the librarian's "correct" response to this program.

Opinion has been as divided as debate has been heated, with ethical issues remaining unresolved, since such issues frequently involve the conflict between one's professional responsibilities and one's responsibilities as a United States citizen.

The FBI program is a highly visible controversy that raises ethical concerns. It has become prominent because today's automated systems are capable of gathering comprehensive data on the use of library materials, which can be used by others for purposes not originally intended. A possible conflict between individual privacy and the need for information may then arise.

Ethics have been brought into prominence by the Freedom of Information Act (FOIA) and related activities of the FBI in our libraries. Many librarians have been offended by the audacity of the government in its efforts to obtain information officials deem important to national security. Particularly disturbing is the demand for this information while those who seek it plainly ignore federal and state statutes. But ambiguous language hinders librarians and information professionals from knowing just where their duty lies. The code of ethics calls for maintenance of "the highest level of personal integrity and competence," but whether we may infer from this that the librarian's ethical action, when requested by federal officials to help identify "foreign nationals," is to cooperate fully or to resist, is unclear, particularly in the light of professional standards and procedures.

The FBI's Library Awareness Program involves FBI agents visiting libraries to request assistance in monitoring library use by "foreigners." Agents of the FBI, in conversations with librarians, frequently define foreigners as people speaking with accents. Millions of foreign-born United States citizens would then warrant government surveillance, because they pronounce words with foreign accents. If it were universally true that this makes them "suspicious," some prominent persons in the highest levels of government would merit strict surveillance: Henry Kissinger and Zbigniew Brzezinski, both national security advisers to recent presidents. In keeping with this policy, their European accents could brand them as potential spies.

More important is the question of what right the FBI, or any government agency, has to know or even to *ask*, what we read, what we study, or what we see? The ALA has invoked the Freedom of Information Act to bring suit against the FBI to obtain full documentation regarding the Library Awareness Program. The issue remains unresolved.

- Ethical problems may be everyday, on-the-job matters of personal conscience, sound management, and common sense. A recent case study, plausible yet fictitious, raises some interesting work-related ethical questions for discussion by information professionals.[33]

- In this case study, a library employee contracts AIDS and, eventually, tells the director. Must or should the rest of the staff be told? Should the public be warned? Does the institution have a higher obligation to the individual employee or to the staff? Should the employee receive counseling? Does long-term illness mean loss of job? Is it ethical to terminate such an employee? Is a severance check in order? Is the individual entitled to pension rights?

This scenario may be one that directors and other administrative personnel will experience all too often in the future and it is important to consider the issues involved carefully before such decisions are required. How we handle these situations will say more about ourselves as librarians, as professionals, and as ethical human beings than it will about library policies.

- If the institution does indeed have an overriding obligation to the individual to respect his privacy, while adhering to his wishes in how the illness is to be handled, should the illness not be treated the same as if cancer, or some other serious malady, had been contracted? If there is no stigma attached to the cancer victim, should any attach to the AIDS sufferer? Would you feel the need to tell other employees if one of your staff were having a mastectomy or a prostate operation?

- Does the public have a right or a need to know about an employee's health problems? Ask yourself whether and how library patrons will be directly affected in answering this question.

- Should the employee be removed involuntarily from contact with clients, unless or until his health should fail to the point that service to the client is impaired or is given in a manner which is no longer accurate, helpful, or efficient? And should such a change in service environment be grounds for dismissal from employment?

Client Confidentiality and the Librarian

Ethical problems directly related to the work itself also arise, such as in reference service.

- Is information gleaned from reference interviews private?

- Does our knowledge of, and friendship for, a client jeopardize the privacy and/or confidentiality of the question/problem and resulting information/responses?

The code of ethics states that we will protect the privacy of our clients. The same principle of privacy which we respect in journalists who will not reveal their sources of information, in medical personnel, who are sworn to confidentiality regarding the health of their patients, in lawyers in their attorney-client relationships, in psychologists who take great pains to maintain a physician-patient relationship, and in the clergy who treat confessions as confidential information, should also be applied to library and information services. There is a difference, however, and it is one of degree. Whereas lawyers and physicians may face legal suits should they reveal identities or confidential information, it is unlikely that librarians would face the same fate— possible, but still unlikely. In addition, malpractice, always a threat for other professionals, has entered the library environment.[34]

- As another example, how should a teacher or school librarian, who discovers in a reference interview that a young client has been physically or sexually abused, treat that information? It is covered under our ethical imperatives and thus is part of the librarian-client relationship. Or do we have a stronger imperative to intervene lest further abuse ensue? Is more abuse, or even a life-threatening situation, likely to occur? Where and when do we cross the line between personal and professional ethics ... or should we?

- What should a librarian do upon suspecting that a depressed and distraught-looking young person, who has requested a book which may be used as a step-by-step, how-to-do-it manual for committing suicide, has more than intellectual curiosity in mind?[35]

- What should be done about the sinister-looking individual who wants reference materials on the construction and use of explosives resulting in a bomb "big enough to blow up a small suburban house?"[36]

  In dealing with clients, must we always be aware of the possibility of legal liability? As stated earlier, the legal and ethical aspects of many problem situations intertwine.[37] Our ethics state that we should treat all cases as confidential, unless permission has been given to discuss, report, or write about the instance. This information should be obtained in writing to protect both the librarian and the library.[38]

- In instances where criminal intent, personal harm, or mass danger is possible, what steps should the information professional take to be on the safe side? Whose advice should be sought?

More common are instances of privacy concerning circulation of certain materials or information in client files.

- Routinely, we are asked for materials which we discover are in the hands of other clients and not due back within a span of time which is suitable for the inquirer. Are there exceptions to our rules?

- Do we, as academic librarians, react in the same way to the request of the provost or dean who wants a source that is on loan to a graduate assistant in the college of education as we would to that of a young college student asking for material checked out to another student?[39]

Law enforcement officials, federal agencies, and members of the journalistic profession have frequently called upon librarians to divulge the identity of a library patron, or, perhaps, a specific individual's borrowing or viewing habits.[40] Ironically, these same individuals or agencies may cite the Freedom of Information Act in requesting the information and as a rationale for violating the rights of others.

- At what point does the right to privacy of the client conflict with the right of others to information? Here again, the distinction between the ethical, "right" thing to do and the legal, permissible thing becomes blurred.[41]

- Do parents have the right to access to public or school library circulation records of their children? For example, do parents have the right to find out whether their children are borrowing books on abortion, or witchcraft, or erotic adventures, or catalogs of homoerotic photographs?

- If there are circumstances in which the library must disclose or provide requested information, what evidence that the requestor has observed legal policy should be required?[42]

- Is it ethically easier to resist enforcement officials when the librarian realizes that he, not the requesting officer, will be liable to lawsuits if the information is surrendered in a manner that violates clients' personal privacy and confidentiality?

Other Ethical Issues

The literature of library/information provision is full of complicated and vexing ethical issues, and related legal ones. Following is a sample of these problems:

- Do we have the right to photocopy? If so, for what purpose and in what quantity? Copyright law is not so specific that all parties to copying will have a clear understanding of what is permissible and what constitutes infringement.

- Many technology-related ethical considerations have arisen from the proliferation of microcomputers and software. But at what point are we "guilty" of plagiarism, theft, or even "software piracy" as a result of copying a program, even if no one else ever finds out?

- Is charging for services in tax-supported, not-for-profit libraries unethical? Which services may we supply at cost, if it is not?

- What ethical considerations should govern the decision of a library staff member who knows that a colleague is a covert drug user? Is there a higher responsibility to protect that person's secret, or is it meritorious to be a "whistleblower" in the interest of public safety? Is it more or less ethical to be cast in the role of "enabler" who knows that the colleague practices an illegal and unsafe habit but remains silent?

- Special librarians in corporations dealing in stocks and bonds frequently come into possession of sensitive, privileged, or "insider" information. In recent years, several persons have been sent to prison for possessing such information, but what ethical considerations govern their behavior regarding this information, both during and after working hours?

- Dealing with vendors and other suppliers of library information is complex and fraught with ethical problems. How can a librarian ensure that he is acting responsibly, yet fulfilling the provisions of a contractual agreement? What is the proper response when a vendor offers to buy lunch or dinner? What about an offer of no-strings, free books or videos, as "gifts for you and your family?"

- How should a librarian act when under attack by those seeking censorship of literature or other library materials? Is it easier to reject library material when one's personal value system or beliefs are at odds with the material being challenged by those demanding censorship?

- Rapid population growth of minority groups in various areas raises issues of how much of the library's budget should be allocated to the support or minority interests and related collections and services. How does this affect the time-honored principle of "a balanced collection?"[43]

Ethics are generally thought to be attitudes generated from beliefs, norms, and experiences. Some are conventions that most societies agree upon, while others are so individual and idiosyncratic that they defy commonality. Ethics are situational, and beliefs or actions differ according to the circumstances of the occasion. The librarian may overlook a minor infraction of the rules on a day when the sun is shining or when his mood is cheery, while enforcing it rigorously on a depressing day or one with stormy weather. On the other hand, inclement weather may incline the librarian to let homeless sleepers rest in one of the library's armchairs, while on a clear day the librarian may feel more like sending them on their way. This question may be one of ethics or of interpersonal differences, but it should be considered in its ethical sense for its implications.

More important ethical questions confront the librarian. Suppose you are an information professional, working in a library setting. Is it right or wrong for you to:

- Give minimal or no service or assistance to high school students doing homework assignments because you feel they would derive more benefit from finding their own information? In school situations this may be a matter of educational pedagogy, but how about in public libraries?

- Refuse to answer questions or to provide information about controversial subjects (e.g., abortion, gay rights, AIDS testing, construction of explosive devices) because of strongly held negative personal beliefs?

- Download from online search services, reformat and repackage the information, and make use of it for profit?

- Copy videocassettes or library-owned computer software for your own private use?

- Take newly accessioned books home before giving the public access to them?

- Give preferential treatment to certain patrons because of status, friendship, or affinity?

- Refuse to acquire certain library materials based on personal principles or views?

- Distribute partisan political campaign literature or display candidates' posters, buttons, or bumper stickers?

- Recommend a personal physician, attorney, computer store, or restaurant?[44]

- Suppose you, as librarian, are invited to go on an expense-paid trip to a book jobber's operation in a distant city? What are the ethical aspects of accepting?

- Suppose a library director is incompetent and the staff knows about it, while the library board seems not to be aware of the fact? Should something be said?

- What if a personal friend of an information professional comes in just before closing time and wants to borrow some materials or equipment that does not circulate from the library? Is it acceptable to make an exception based on friendship and the belief that you can trust that individual to return the borrowed items before anyone notices?

For most librarians, honest answers to these questions would probably be along the lines of "Well, it depends...." Honesty compels most of us to avoid clear-cut, black-and-white positions and to allow mitigating circumstances and individual cases to dictate likely courses of action.

Ethics, therefore, are not legal matters, although legal consequences can and do ensue from matters of personal temperament, personality, and judgment. Ethics are very much personal sets of values, which vary from time to time and from place to place, unlike morals, which tend to be deep-seated and not as subject to change with circumstances.

Some lists of ethical dilemmas go considerably beyond the judgments or circumstances of the moment. The ALA's Committee on Professional Ethics cites *The Librarian's Code of Ethics* and describes a few dilemmas that are as hard to define as they are to resolve:[45]

- One interesting case involves "skip tracers," who are hired by credit collection bureaus to locate and dun persons who move and leave no forwarding address while owing money. To locate such elusive individuals, skip tracers frequently resort to address-ordered city directories ("criss-cross" directories) on the assumption that calling the neighbors of the "skips" will frequently lead to their whereabouts. Should the librarian refuse to assist the client because of disapproval of the caller's intentions or methods? Is there any justification for requesting that the caller state the reason for the request? Does it make a difference whether we are certain that the caller is a skip tracer or only an old friend trying to track down a past acquaintance? Should the library decline to purchase such directories because of potential uses of their contents? Here, the legal ramifications are subordinate to the ethical ones.

   In general, it is wrong for a librarian, working in a publicly supported institution established for the purpose of providing information to the public on demand, to refuse to provide any available information? As before, the honest answer is along the lines of "It depends...."

- "Budgetary censorship" is another gray area of ethical concern. A library may cite limited resources and higher priorities as reasons for not buying particular materials or items of a particular type, but what consequences might ensue should such decisions be challenged? Perhaps the worst censors are those with the power to make decisions. Maybe, as Walt Kelly's *Pogo* told us years ago, "We have met the enemy, and he is us."

ETHICS FOR INFORMATION PROFESSIONALS

The American Society for Information Science (ASIS) has developed its own professional code of ethics, which differs little, in overall intention and effect, from that of the ALA, yet which seeks an accommodation between the need of the information professional to adhere to the highest levels of professional integrity and the concomitant need for some members to serve clientele in exchange for financial compensation. Such a situation often develops conflicting responsibilities, leading to very real dilemmas of conflict of interest. For this reason, the elaboration of ethics for information scientists is trickier than that for employees of tax-supported libraries and information centers, who normally need not consider the profit motive in working through their obligations. ASIS is still wrestling with the final language of its code, but its ultimate provisions will not differ appreciably from that found in appendix B of this book.

A footnote to the code informs the reader that it "is not intended as regulatory, with sanctions for those who violate its provisions; rather, it is to provide assistance for members in guiding their activities and in directing their thoughts on the ethical aspects of the profession."[46] That this code sets up a perilous and intricate path for the professional, in which it is frequently difficult, and occasionally impossible, to satisfy one's client, sponsor, or employer and, at the same time, strive for the highest standards of competence, judgment, integrity, and ethical standards, is demonstrable. However, the code is a statement of good intentions and commendable as desirable guidelines, whatever its feasibility and practicality in professional practice for information providers.[47]

Professionalism

Today, the information professional's status is improving steadily and new technological developments may soon augment that status even more. This optimistic forecast is based on the expectation that someday soon, society is going to realize that:

1. People will need information to manage their lives better, or even to manage them at all, in increasing, and increasingly specialized, amounts.

2. Information is growing at a staggering, even frightening, rate. Futurist Frank Ogden estimates that the world's total amount of recorded knowledge is now doubling every twenty months. He posits that everything you learn will be obsolete or outgrown in six months and that 80 percent of what you think you know now is worthless.

3. With all that information around, and given that people will need it more than ever, somebody (somebody who knows how to manage it) will be needed more than ever to collect it, store it, organize it, evaluate it, sift it, make it available in the desired quantities, and get it into people's hands when and where they need it.

4. The person or persons who perform this function better than the general population can, or who perform this function more quickly or effectively, will be highly valued by society and will reap commensurate rewards from that society.

Of course, there is a difference between talking about the library in society and the *librarian* (or information professional) in society, but apparently we, as individuals, share the same fate as our institutions. As information grows in value, society will value more those who do the work of finding information and getting it to the right people, in the right form, and at the right time.

This book cannot provide guidelines or steps to follow when ethical challenges occur; as circumstances behind such challenges vary so widely, it would be impossible to do so. But each reader should spend some time comtemplating the issues presented here, possibly role-playing various parts in the conflicts. This will not likely or necessarily prepare the reader for coming up with the "correct" answers to the questions you may be asked, but at least you will have considered the questions before they are actually posed and you must formulate a response.

It is in the nature of ethical discussions that they raise more questions than they answer. This makes for interesting discussions, but the ultimate "truth" or validity of any decision in which ethical factors play a part lies in the set of circumstances surrounding it, and in the conscience of the decision maker.

NOTES

[1] Alex Ladenson, ed. *American Library Laws*. 5th ed. (Chicago: American Library Association, 1983).

[2] Robert McClarren. "The Marks of a 'Competent' and 'Qualified' Head Librarian." *Illinois Libraries* (October 1984): 415-19.

[3] *American Library Laws*, pp. 186-87.

[4] *Ibid.* p. 261.

[5] Alaska Statute Section 23.10.037; Michigan Comp. Laws Ann Sections 37.201-208; Utah Code Ann Section 34.37-16; Mid-South Hospital 221 NLRB 670 (1975).

[6] "Can You Pass the Job Test?" *Newsweek* (May 5, 1986): 46.

[7] *New York Times*, March 5, 1986, p. A-1-a.

[8] *Ibid.*, pp. 48-49.

[9] *Hollenbaugh v. Carnegie Free Library*, NLRB 815 (1978).

[10] Keith M. Cottam. "Affirmative Action: Attitude Makes a Difference." *Library Journal* 112 (May 15, 1987): 47-50.

[11] *Ibid.*

[12] Barbara B. Moran. "The Impact of Affirmative Action on Academic Libraries." *Library Trends* (Fall 1985): 199-217.

[13] "Women Librarians Document 'Inequities' in Ohio." *American Libraries* (June 1987): 412.

[14] *Ibid.*

[15] Jo Cates. "Sexual Harassment: What Every Woman and Man Should Know." *Library Journal* (July 1985): 23-29. See also A. J. Anderson's case study, "I'm Being Sexually Harassed." *Library Journal* (May 15, 1986): 44-47.

[16] Michigan Task Force on Sexual Harassment in the Workplace. (Lansing, Mich.: Michigan Equal Employment Commission, 1986).

[17] *McKinney v. Dole*, 765 F.2d 1129 (D.C. Cir. 1985).

[18] Alan Lincoln. *Crime in the Library* (New York: R. R. Bowker, 1984), p. 19.

[19] *Ibid.*, p. 20.

[20] William W. McCullough. *Sticky Fingers: A Close Look at America's Fastest-Growing Crime* (New York: Amacom, 1981), p. 1.

[21] Lawrence R. Zeitlin. "A Little Larceny Can Do a Lot for Employee Morale." *Psychology Today* (June 1971): 22-26, 64.

[22] See *New York Times*, September 18, 1987, p. 1 and "FBI Asks Librarians to Eye Foreigners; IFC Responds." *American Libraries* (November 1987): 812-14.

[23] A number of readily available case studies assist students and librarians with formulating responses to "problem patron situations." See, for example, A. J. Anderson. "To Catch a Thief?" *Library Journal* (March 1, 1984): 449-52, or Bruce A. Shuman, "Job Testing," in *River Bend in Transition: Managing Change in Public Libraries* (Phoenix, Ariz.: Oryx Press, 1987), pp. 114-18.

[24] The Federal Family Education Records Privacy Act (FERPA) provides access to the records of minor children. Section 438, dealing with protection of the rights and privacy of parents and students, states: "No funds shall be made available under any applicable program to any educational agency or institution which has a policy of denying, or which effectively prevents, the parents of students who are or have been in attendance at a school of such agency or at such institution, as the case may be, the right to inspect and review the educational records of their children."

[25] "Smelly People Barred from Ann Arbor Public Library." *Library Journal* (February 1, 1985): 19.

[26] See "How Companies Avoid Mistakes in Hiring: Sophisticated Tests Are Joining Other Methods of Screening Job Applicants." *Nation's Business* 73 (June 1985): 34-37; "The Gene Screen: Genetic Screening of Employees." *Inc.* (April 1984): 55-57; and "Can You Pass the Job Test?" *Newsweek* (May 5, 1986): 46-53.

[27] Mary Hutchings Reed. "Employment Discrimination and Related Litigation in Libraries." *Journal of Library Administration* (Winter 1986): 53-66.

[28] A pertinent article on collective bargaining is "Statement on Academic Government for Institutions Engaged in Collective Bargaining." *Academe* 73 (November/December 1987): 25-26. Intended for academic institutions, it can be applied to other environments.

[29] See Karen K. Niemeyer, "Copyright and Technology," in *School Library Media Annual 4, 1986*, ed. by Shirley L. Aaron and Pat R. Scales (Littleton, Colo.: Libraries Unlimited, Inc., 1986), pp. 22-39; William T. McGrath. "Piracy of Intellectual Property: A Report of the International Piracy Project." *Bulletin of the American Society for Information Science* (February/March 1990): 9-13. and Virginia Helm. *What Educators Should Know about Copyright* (Bloomington, Ind.: Phi Delta Kappa Educational Foundation, 1986). ERIC ED 279-329.

[30] Ann E. Prentice. "Professional Ethics." *Catholic Library World* 56 (November 1984): 180-83.

[31] *Intellectual Freedom Manual* 3d ed. (Chicago: American Library Association, 1989).

[32] "The Freedom of Information Act" (5 U.S.C. 552, as amended), in U.S. Department of Justice, *Freedom of Information Case List* (Washington, D.C.: Government Printing Office, 1988). See also Richard M. Schmidt, Jr. and Robert Clifton Burns. "The Freedom of Information Act: An Overview for Librarians," in *Legal Issues for Library and Information Managers*, ed. by William Z. Nasri (New York: Haworth Press, 1987), pp. 9-17.

[33] A. J. Anderson. "Crisis at the WPL: Dan Has AIDS." *Library Journal* (September 15, 1988): 59-60.

[34] Thomas Steele. "The Liability of Librarians for Negligence." *Public Libraries* (Fall 1987): 127-28.

[35] Books on this topic actually exist: see Claude Guillon. *Suicide: Mode d'emploi: Histoire, technique, actualité* [Suicide Operating Instructions] (Paris: A. Moreau, 1982); Derek Humphrey. *Final Exit* (Los Angeles: Hemlock/Carol, 1991).

[36] Robert Hauptman. "Professionalism or Culpability? An Experiment in Ethics." *Wilson Library Bulletin* (April 1976): 626-27. Of thirteen librarians queried, not one refused to supply information on ethical grounds. See also these other articles on the treatment of problem patrons: A. J. Anderson. "The Trouble with Larry." *Library Journal* (June 15, 1986): 45-47; J. Kirk Brashear, James J. Maloney, and Judellen Thorton-Jaringe. "Problem Patrons: The Other Kind of Library Security." *Illinois Libraries* (April 1981): 343-51. For relevant case studies, see Bruce A. Shuman. *River Bend Revisited: The Problem Patron in the Library* (Phoenix, Ariz.: Oryx Press, 1984).

37 Joseph J. Mika and Bruce A. Shuman. "Legal Issues Affecting Libraries and Librarians." *American Libraries* 19 (February 1988): 108, 111-12.

38 William Z. Nasri. "Malpractice Liability: Myth or Reality." *Journal of Library Administration* (Winter 1980): 3-6.

39 Mika and Shuman, "Legal Issues."

40 Mark Stover. "Confidentiality and Privacy in Reference Service." *RQ* 27 (Winter 1987): 240-44. See also Robin K. Mills. "Reference Service vs. Legal Advice." *Law Library Journal* 72 (1979): 179-93.

41 Anne P. Mintz. "Information Practice and Malpractice." *Library Journal* (September 15, 1985): 38-43. See also Mary Prokop and Charles R. McClure. "The Public Librarian and Service Ethics: A Dilemma." *Public Library Quarterly* (Winter 1982): 69-81.

42 For example, after John Hinckley, Jr.'s attempted assassination of President Ronald Reagan in 1981, his hometown library (Jefferson County Library, Lakewood, Colorado) was directed by the county attorney to hand over Hinckley's borrowing records, which revealed that Hinckley had borrowed *The Fan*, a suspense novel by Bob Randall, in which a young man's infatuation and obsession with an actress (like Hinckley's with Jodie Foster) leads to violence. See also Susan Dunn. "Society, Information Needs, Library Services & Liability." *Iowa Library Quarterly* 26, no. 3 (1989): 18-20, which suggests that the public is increasingly aware of its legal rights and "Patrons now know they have a right to accurate information and a right to sue because of actions taken on the advice of librarians or based on library data that proves faulty."

43 American Library Association. *Intellectual Freedom Manual.* 3d ed. (Chicago: American Library Association, 1989).

44 Terry W. Cole. "Legal Issues and Censorship Cases." *School Library Media Quarterly* (Spring 1985): 115-22.

45 American Library Association, Committee on Professional Ethics. *Ethics Sin List.* (American Library Association, 1987).

46 *Intellectual Freedom Manual.*

47 Manfred Kochen. "Ethics and Information Science." *Journal of the American Society for Information Science* (May 1987): 206-10.

REFERENCE LIST

Legal Issues

Falsone, Anne Marie. "Privacy of Circulation Files." *Journal of Library Administration* (Winter 1986): 19-23.

Galvin, Thomas J., and Sally Mason. "Videos, Libraries, and the Law: Finding the Balance. *American Libraries* 20 (February 1989): 110-19.

Mika, Joseph J., and Bruce A. Shuman. "Legal Issues Affecting Libraries and Librarians." (A tutorial course covering both legal and ethical concerns of information professionals.) *American Libraries* 19 (January-April 1988).

Million, Angela C., and Kim N. Fisher. "Library Records: A Review of Confidentiality Laws and Policies." *Journal of Academic Librarianship* (January 1986): 346-49.

Nasri, William Z. "Copyright." In *ALA World Encyclopedia of Library and Information Services*. 2d ed., pp. 223-30. Chicago: American Library Association, 1986.

_____. *Legal Issues for Library and Information Managers*. New York: Haworth Press, 1987.

Schmidt, Richard M., Jr., and Robert Clifton Burns. "The Freedom of Information Act: An Overview for Librarians." In William Z. Nasri, ed., *Legal Issues for Library and Information Managers*. New York: Haworth Press, 1987. pp. 9-17.

Swan, John C. "Public Records and Library Privacy." *Library Journal* (September 1, 1983): 1645-50.

_____. "Untruth or Consequences." *Library Journal* (July 1986): 44-52.

Ethical Issues

Allison, Anne Marie. "Ethics, Yes! Enforcement, No ... Or Maybe?" *Library Administration and Management* 1 (January 1987): 8-15.

Capurro, Rafael. "Moral Issues in Information Science." *Journal of Information Science* 11 (Spring 1987): 113-23.

Dizard, Wilson P., Jr. *The Coming Information Age*. 3d ed. New York: Longman Publishing, 1989.

Finks, Lee W. "Librarianship Needs a New Code of Ethics." *American Libraries* 22 (January 1991): 84-92.

_____. "Values Without Shame." *American Libraries* 20 (April 1989): 352-56.

Hauptman, Robert. *Ethical Challenges in Librarianship*. Phoenix, Ariz.: Oryx Press, 1988.

Lindsey, Jonathan A., and Ann E. Prentice. *Professional Ethics and Librarians*. Phoenix, Ariz.: Oryx Press, 1988.

"On Professional Ethics." *American Libraries* 12 (June 1981): 335.

Peterson, Kenneth G. "This Is Academic Librarianship: The Need for Values." *Journal of Academic Librarianship* 9 (July 1983): 132-37.

Appendix A
The Librarian's Code of Ethics*

THE LIBRARIAN'S CODE OF ETHICS

I.   Librarians must provide the highest level of service through appropriate and usefully organized collections, fair and equitable circulation and service policies, and skillful, accurate, unbiased, and courteous responses to all requests for assistance.

II. Librarians must resist all efforts by groups or individuals to censor library materials.

III. Librarians must protect each user's right to privacy with respect to information sought or received and materials consulted, borrowed, or acquired.

IV. Librarians must adhere to the principles of due process and equality of opportunity in peer relationships and personal actions.

V.   Librarians must distinguish clearly in their actions and statements between their personal philosophies and attitudes and those of an institution or professional body.

VI. Librarians must avoid situations in which personal interests might be served or financial benefits gained at the expense of library users, colleagues, or the employing institution.

Intellectual Freedom Manual 3d ed. (Chicago: American Library Association, 1989).

Appendix B
A Code of Ethics for
Information Scientists *

Responsibility to Individual Persons

Information professionals should:

- strive to make information available to individuals who need it

- strive both to ensure accuracy and not to infringe upon privacy or confidentiality in providing information about individuals

- protect each information user's and provider's right to privacy and confidentiality

- respect an information provider's proprietary rights

Responsibility to Society

Information professionals should:

- serve the legitimate information needs of a large and complex society while at the same time being mindful of individuals' rights

- resist efforts to censor publications

- play active roles in educating society to understand and appreciate the importance of information promoting equal opportunity for access to information

_____

*Bulletin of the American Society for Information Science (August/September 1990): 25.

Responsibility to the Sponsor, Client or Employer

Information professionals should:

- strive to serve the interests of the sponsor

- maintain confidentiality of background or product information and strictly observe nondisclosure agreements

- avoid a conflict of interest or appearance of such among sponsors

- refuse requests of an ethically questionable nature and inform sponsors of their objections

Responsibility to the Profession

Information professionals should:

- perform professional services in a manner so as to enhance the profession, which must earn and keep the respect of individuals, of its sponsors, and of its society

- avoid situations in which personal interests might be served or financial benefits gained inappropriately

- adhere to the principles of due process and equality of opportunity in peer relationships and personnel actions

- cultivate awareness of the ethical implications of their professional activities and promote public discussion of ethical issues

Index

AASL. *See* American Association of School Librarians

Academic libraries, 52-73

Access
to information, 21, 112
to libraries, 36

Accountability, 38

Accreditation, 96
of libraries, 60
of library science programs, 96, 133

Acquisitions, 69

Activist function of libraries, 31

Administration and management of libraries. *See* Personnel

Advice, 84-85, 116-17

Advocacy, 84-85, 116-17

Affirmative action. *See* Discrimination, employment

Afterschool programs, 93

AI. *See* Artificial intelligence

AIDS, 152-53. *See also* Privacy.

ALA. *See* American Library Association

Alcohol abuse. *See* Drug and alcohol abuse

Alexandrian Library. *See* Egypt, libraries

American Association of School Librarians, 90, 96

American Library Association (ALA), 2, 89, 95, 113, 137
Committee on Accreditation (COA), 96
Office for Intellectual Freedom, 121-22

American Library Laws, 133

American Society for Information Science (ASIS), 158-59

Archival functions of libraries, 27, 43

Archives, 43

Artificial intelligence (AI), 22

ASIS. *See* American Society for Information Science

Associations for librarians. *See professional associations*

Association of College and Research Libraries (ACRL), 60, 95

Association of Research Libraries (ARL), 60

Audiences. *See* Users of libraries

Audiovisual services in libraries. *See* Media in libraries

Automation of library processes and services, 16, 19, 58, 68, 107, 113-14

Availability of other libraries, 67

Balanced collection, 69

Ballard, Thomas H., 72, 114

Barriers to library services, 57-61

Bequests as a source of funding, 65. *See also* Funding for libraries

Bond issues. *See* Funding for libraries

Bookmobiles, 81-82

Books by mail, 83

Bradford, Samuel C., 16

Branch libraries, 81

British Museum, 14

Budget allocations, 57-59

Business libraries. *See* Special libraries

Carnegie, Andrew, 15. *See also* Philanthropy

Catalogs, 36-37. *See also* Online catalogs

CD-ROM, 22. *See also* Databases

Censorship, 14, 120-23. *See also* Intellectual freedom

Centralization of library services. *See* Diversification of library services

Certain, Charles C., 89

Change agent, library as, 31-32

Change and libraries, xiii, 68

Children's services, 93

Citation analysis, 18

Civil Rights Act (1964), 138

Clapp-Jordan formula, 56, 69. *See also* Collection development

Clerical positions. *See* Personnel, library

COA. *See* American Library Association, Committee on Accreditation

Collection development, 69

Collective bargaining. *See* Unions in libraries

College and Research Libraries, 60